I0528322

10 9 8 7 6 5 4 3 2 1

ISBN-13: 978-1-964243-64-1
ISBN 10: 1-964243-64-1

Permission request(s) should be submitted to the publisher in writing at one of the addresses below:

CHEETAH® Toys & More, LLC
207 Main Street, 3rd Floor
Hartford, CT 06106

Trowers Enterprises Limited
Kampala, Uganda
Cheetahuganda@gmail.com

info@mycheetahinc.com
paulettetrowers@yahoo.com
WhatsApp: 876-909-6311

Authors: Kristina Jaz; Iain Taylor; Paulette Trowers, Juris Doctor
Editors: Fiona Porter-Lawson; Yanique Wallace
Reviewers: Ministry of Education & Youth related personnel; Janice Trowers, MSED, Curriculum Specialist

Cover and interior design: CHEETAH® Purrrrrrr Publishing ("CHEETAH®"), an imprint of CHEETAH® Toys & More, LLC.
Publisher: CHEETAH® (Connect to Higher Education, Electronic Tools, Application & Help)

This book belongs to:

Name:

....

School:

....

Date:

....

Table of Contents

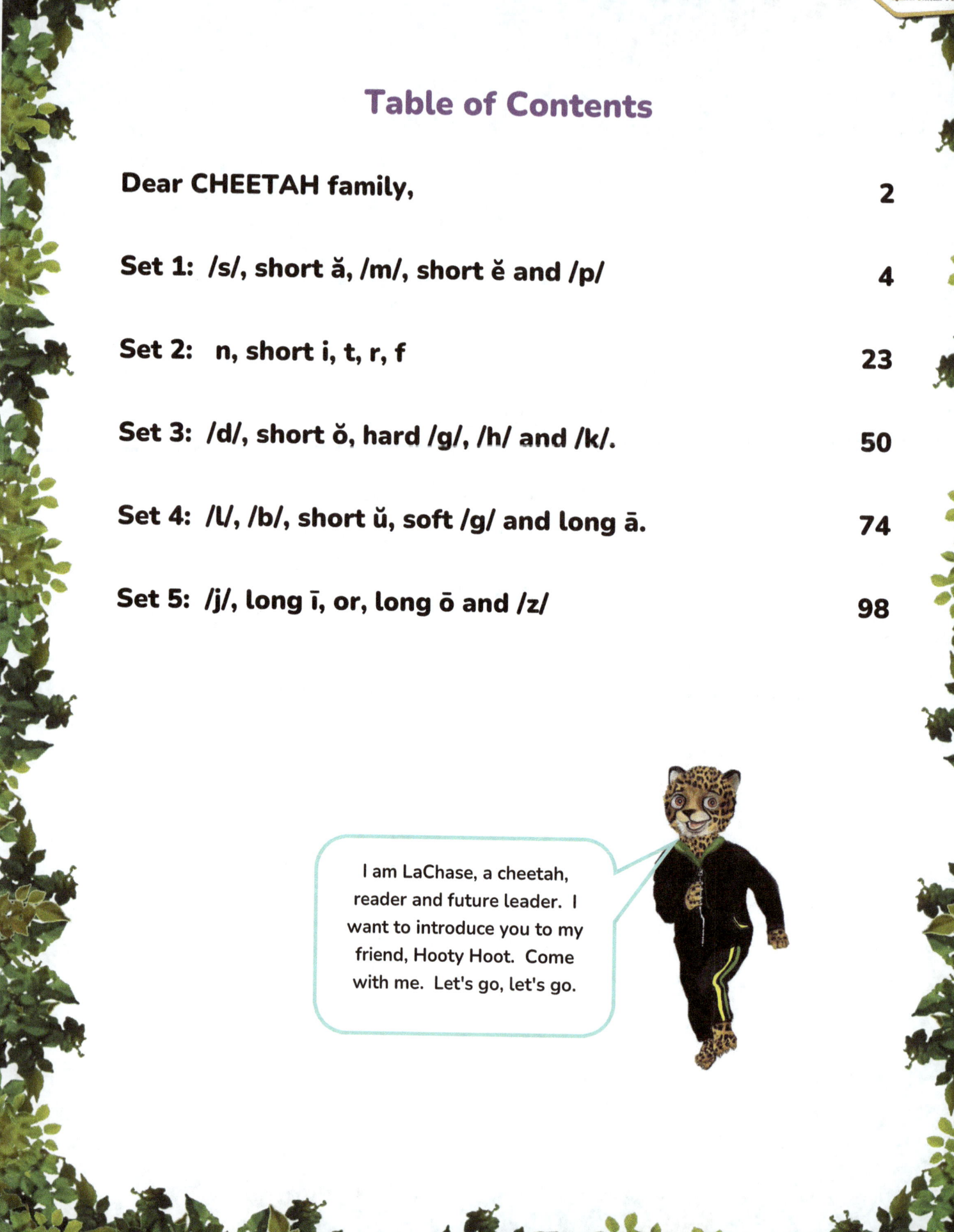

I am LaChase, a cheetah, reader and future leader. I want to introduce you to my friend, Hooty Hoot. Come with me. Let's go, let's go.

Dear CHEETAH family,

As you teach each sound, the lesson format will follow the CHEETAH® CAPE tool.

Teach me and I will learn.

CONCEPT (exploration) sections give the information and knowledge the pupil needs to understand the lesson fully. Look at the letter that represents the phonic sound and practise making the sound together. Use the story and its action to hear the letter sound in context. Show the pupil where the phonic sound can appear in a word. Say the words in the word bank together and use the story to find more words with the focus sound.

Show me and I will follow.

This symbol shows sections to be read by the adult.
Using instruments and the CHEETAH train song lyrics is another way for auditory learners to further explore the sound.

APPLY (elaboration) sections ask the pupil to apply the information they have learned to solve problems.

Let me do it and I will not forget.

PRACTICE (further elaboration) sections allow the pupil to use the information and skills they have learned during fun activities that are guided by the teacher.

How am I doing?

EVALUATE (self-reflection) sections are a chance for the teacher and parent to communicate and keep track of the pupil's understanding of key concepts. Pupils get a chance to express their feelings. This is also where the pupil, parent or guardian will be given stickers to celebrate their learning!

Clusters for Teaching Phonemes

Set 1: s, (short) a, m, (short) e, p

Set 2: f, n, (short) i, t, r

Set 3: d, (short) o, g, h, c/k

Set 4: l, b, (short) u, g, (long) a

Set 5: j, (long) i, or, (long) o, z

Set 6: ng, w/wh, oo/oo, v

Set 7: ch, sh, (long) e, th(voiced),th(unvoiced), y

Set 8: x, qu, oi, (long) u, ar

Set 9: ow/ou, zh, er

Set 1

/s/, short ă, /m/, short ĕ and /p/

Here are some C-DER books to read:

Sound	C-DER reference	Book title
s	Set 1, Book 3	*At the Farm*
short a	Set 1, Book 1	*Meet My Family*
m	Set 6, Book 52	*Mr. Pete Makes Friends*
short e	Set 3, Book 23	*Off to the Vet*
p	Set 6, Book 48	*House Flood*

Let's read together: At the Farm

Before you begin, use the book to introduce the literary terms 'title' and 'author'.

During the story, point to Sam and ask, *"Who is this character?"* and later, *"What is this character's name?"*

After the story, discuss: *"What other characters are in the story?" "Who is Pam?"*

CHEETAH® train loves a song, zooming as it hums along.
It zooms beside the sea, past a seal swimming free.
Can you guess which sound is next?

Find an instrument, then play and sing along using the lyrics above!
Use your mouth to make my sound!

S is on the way to town.
CHEETAH® train is slowing down.

Ss

Circle the pictures with the /s/ sound.

Practise writing the letter *s*.

Listen then underline all the words in the passage with the /s/ sound.

Mrs. Sun says, "Hello, Sam!"

So, Sam stops to share some stories.

At sunset, they say their sweet goodbyes.

"See you soon Mrs. Sun!"

Colour the face that shows how you feel about the /s/ sound.

Got it! | Almost got it | No, didn't get it

Are you ready to find out what sound is next? Then let's fly!

Dear Parent: Date: ________________

________________ does/does not fully understand the phonic sound /s/. Please continue to review at home.

Signed: ______________________

Dear Teacher: Date:______________

Thank you. We have reviewed the phonic sound /s/ together. My child had a chance to teach me.

Signed: ______________________

Reward sticker for parent or guardian goes here.

Well done!

____

(write name

understands the phonic sound /s/.

Sticker for pupil goes here!

Let's read together: Meet my Family

Before you begin, share the title and ask, *"Who do you think the people on the front cover might be?"*

During the story, ask questions to confirm if the predictions made before reading were correct.

After the story, ask, *"Is your family like this family? Is your family the same or different?"*

CHEETAH® train loves a song, zooming as it hums along.
It zooms across the street. Oh, ants are on the seat.
Can you guess which sound is next?

Find an instrument, then play and sing along using the lyrics above!
Can you make my sound three times?

A is on the way to town.
CHEETAH® train is slowing down.

Say the name of each picture. Colour the pictures with the short ă sound in their name.

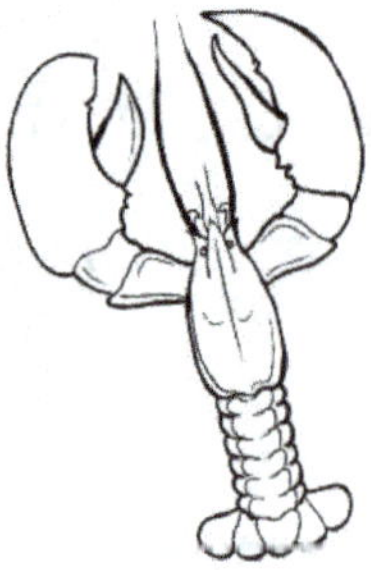

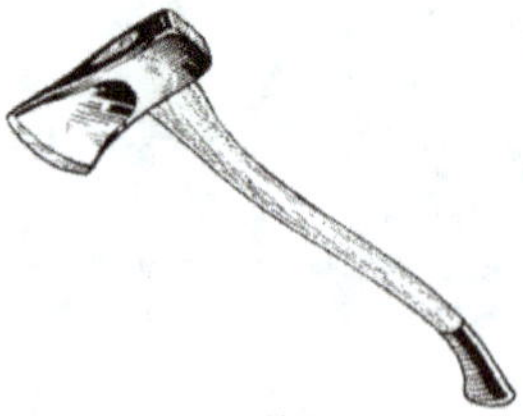

Practise writing the letter *a*.

Listen then circle the words in the passage with the short ă sound.

"I am an ant," says Anna the ant.

Anna has an apple.

The apple is as big as Anna!

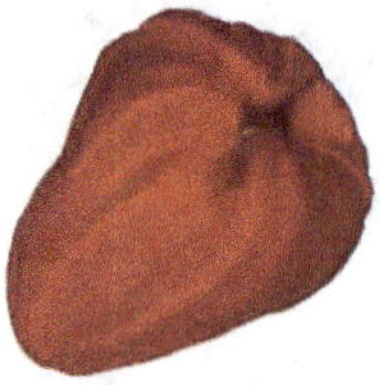

Anna says, "Can ant eat apples?"

"We can eat an apple a day," the ants say.

Colour the face that shows how you feel about the short ă sound.

Got it! | Almost got it | No, didn't get it

You are doing very well! Come, let us soar to the next page.

Dear Parent: Date: ________________

______________ does/does not fully understand the phonic sound short ă. Please continue to review at home.

Signed: ______________________

Dear Teacher: Date:_____________

Thank you. We have reviewed the phonic sound short ă together. My child had a chance to teach me.

Signed: ____________________

Reward sticker for parent or guardian goes here.

Well done!

____

(write name here)

understands the phonic sound short ă.

Sticker for pupil goes here!

Let's read together: Mr. Pete Makes Friends

Before you begin, share the title and ask, "*What do you think might happen in this story?*"

During the story, after each page of text, ask, "*What do you think might happen next?*"

After the story ask, "*What was the problem in this story? How was the problem solved?*"

CHEETAH® train loves a song, zooming as it hums along.
It zooms across the map, while Monkey Mike takes a nap.
Can you guess which letter sound is next?

Find an instrument, then play and sing along using the lyrics above!
Put your lips together to make my sound!

M is on the way to town.
CHEETAH® train is slowing down.

Mm

Circle the word that matches each picture.

man  ant

bus  map

sand  drum

Practise writing the letter *m*.

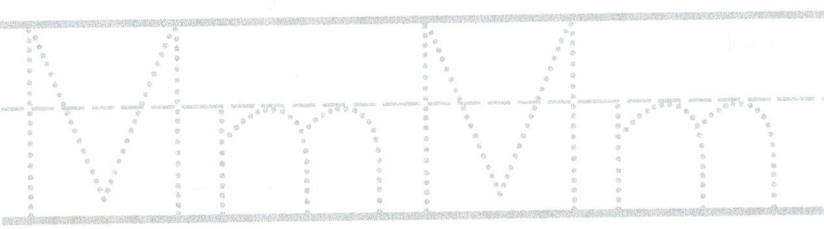

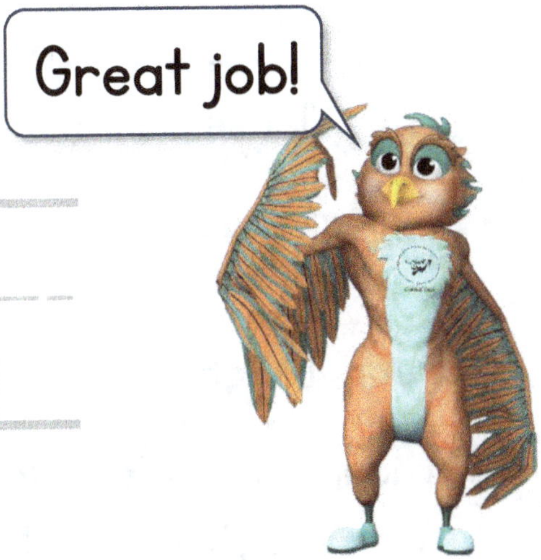

Listen then <u>underline</u> the words in the passage with the */m/* sound.

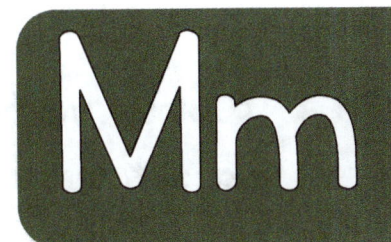

Mike is a monkey with many maps.

The map shows Mike Jamaica.

He follows some mountains.

"Max! Use your map. Don't miss the mark!"

Colour the face that shows how you feel about the /m/ sound.

Got it! Almost got it No, didn't get it

Learning is an adventure. Let us continue together!

Dear Parent: Date: ________________

_______________ does/does not fully understand the phonic sound /m/. Please continue to review at home.

Signed: ______________________

Dear Teacher: Date:______________

Thank you. We have reviewed the phonic sound /m/ together. My child had a chance to teach me.

Signed: _____________________

Reward sticker for parent or guardian goes here.

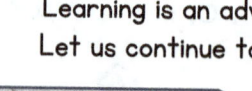

Well done!

____

(write name here)

understands the phonic sound /m/.

Sticker for pupil goes here!

Let's read together: Off to the Vet

Before you begin, share the title and ask, "*Who is a vet? Do you have a pet? Have they ever needed to visit the vet?*"

During the story, point out the words that rhyme and explain why they rhyme.

After the story ask, "*Can you recall two words from the story that rhyme?*" Look back and find more examples together.

CHEETAH® train loves a song, zooming as it hums along.
It zooms across the land, past elephants and yellow sand.
Can you guess which sound is next?

Find an instrument, then play and sing along using the lyrics above!
Look in a mirror as you make my sound!

E is on the way to town.
CHEETAH® train is slowing down.

Ee

Draw lines to match the word to the picture.

vet   egg   hen   web

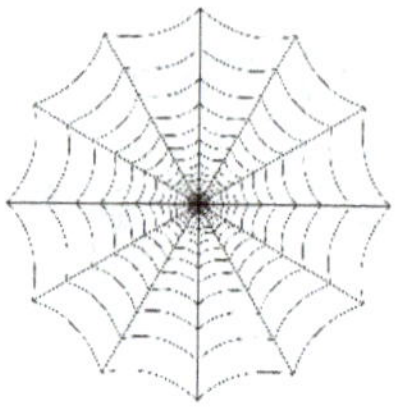

Practise writing the letter *e*.

e e e

Listen then <u>underline</u> all the words in the passage with the /e/ sound.

At the end of the bend, Ted met Ben.

Then, they went to the den.

That is when Ted fed the red hen.

"Let us go to bed, it is very late," said Ted.

Colour the face that shows how you feel about the short ĕ sound.

Got it! | Almost got it | No, didn't get it

You are a CHEETAH, a future leader. Come, let us continue.

Dear Parent: Date: _______________

_______________ does/does not fully understand the phonic sound short ĕ. Please continue to review at home.

Signed: _____________________

Dear Teacher: Date: _____________

Thank you. We have reviewed the phonic sound ĕ together. My child had a chance to teach me.

Signed: _____________________

Reward sticker for parent or guardian goes here.

Well done!

____

(write name here)

understands the phonic sound short ĕ.

Sticker for pupil goes here!

Let's read together: House Flood

Before you begin, share the title and ask, *"What is a flood?"* *"How might a house flood?"* Encourage use of the illustration for clues.

During the story, stop after reading the opening page. Ask, *"What do you think has happened?"* Stop again after reading 'she tiptoes in.' Ask, *"What might happen next? Why do you think this?"*

CHEETAH® train loves a song, zooming as it hums along.
It zooms beside the breeze, as pandas play in the trees.
Can you guess which sound is next?

Find an instrument, then play and sing along using the lyrics above!
Squeeze your lips to make my sound.

P is on the way to town.
CHEETAH® train is slowing down.

Pp

Say the words. Draw a line from the letter *p* to all the pictures with a /p/ sound.

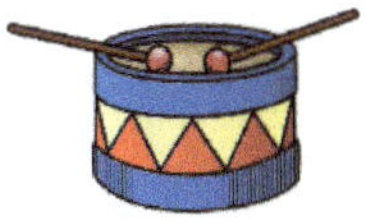

Practise writing the letter *p*.

Listen to the passage. Clap whenever you hear the /p/ sound.

Pip has a pink pet pig.

The pig loves to jump in the mud.

Pip says, "Pet pig! Get up, let us play!"

Pip and his pet have a super time.

Colour the face that shows how you feel about the /p/ sound.

Got it! | Almost got it | No, didn't get it

I believe in you. Let us take off together! Come wid mi!

Dear Parent: Date: ________________

_______________ does/does not fully understand the phonic sound /p/. Please continue to review at home.

Signed: ______________________

Dear Teacher: Date:______________

Thank you. We have reviewed the phonic sound /p/ together. My child had a chance to teach me.

Signed: _____________________

Reward sticker for parent or guardian goes here.

Well done!

____

(write name here)

understands the phonic sound /p/.

Sticker for pupil goes here!

Set 1

CHEETAH's review

Look at each row. Circle the picture that starts with the sound.

s

short a

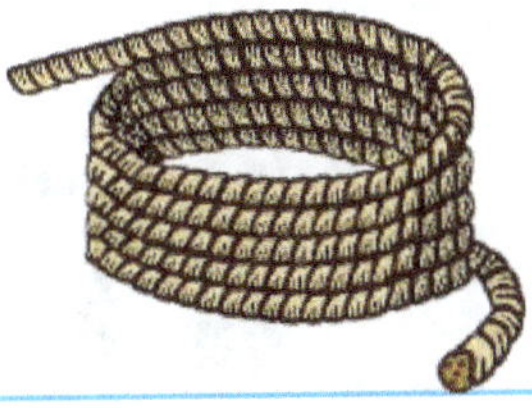

m

short e

p

CHEETAH's review

Use the letters to make as many short /a/ and /e/ words as you can. Letters can be used more than once, and nonsense words are welcome. Be creative and have fun!

p n m a e r s t

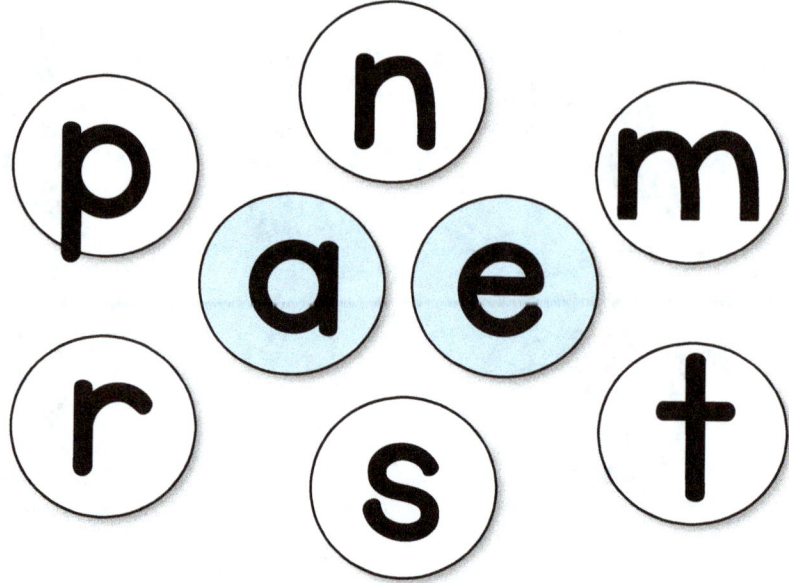

HEETAH®'s review

Find the high frequency words in the wordsearch.

m	a	k	e	m
o	n	s	r	e
m	t	h	i	s
y	p	w	m	a
p	u	t	a	w

put me saw this make my

How did you do? Did you learn anything new? Come, come, let's go! Learning never ends.

Solve the clues to complete the crossword.

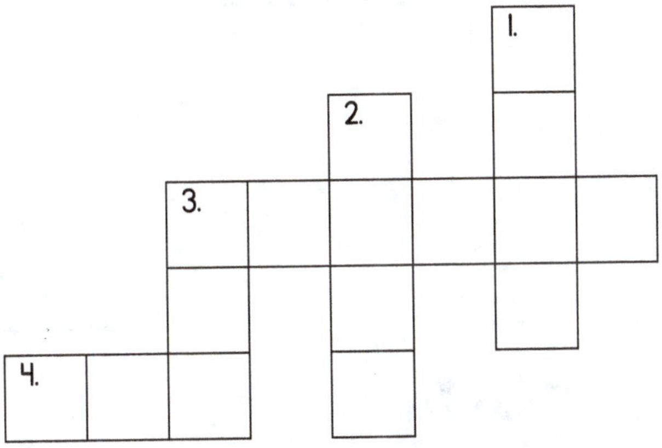

Across:

3. The colour of the sun.
4. The boy ___ red hair.

Down:

1. What cars do at a red traffic light.
2. This is what you do with your toys.
3. The word you say when you agree.

Let's create words

Complete the table. Put the letters together to make words.

Beginning sound	Middle sound	End sound	Words created
s	a	t	sat, set, mat, met, pat, pet
m		m	
p	e	p	

List the words that you do not know the meaning of.

____

____

Ask an adult what they mean.

Let's put together

Connect the boxes to make words from the -am word family. Write them in the given space.

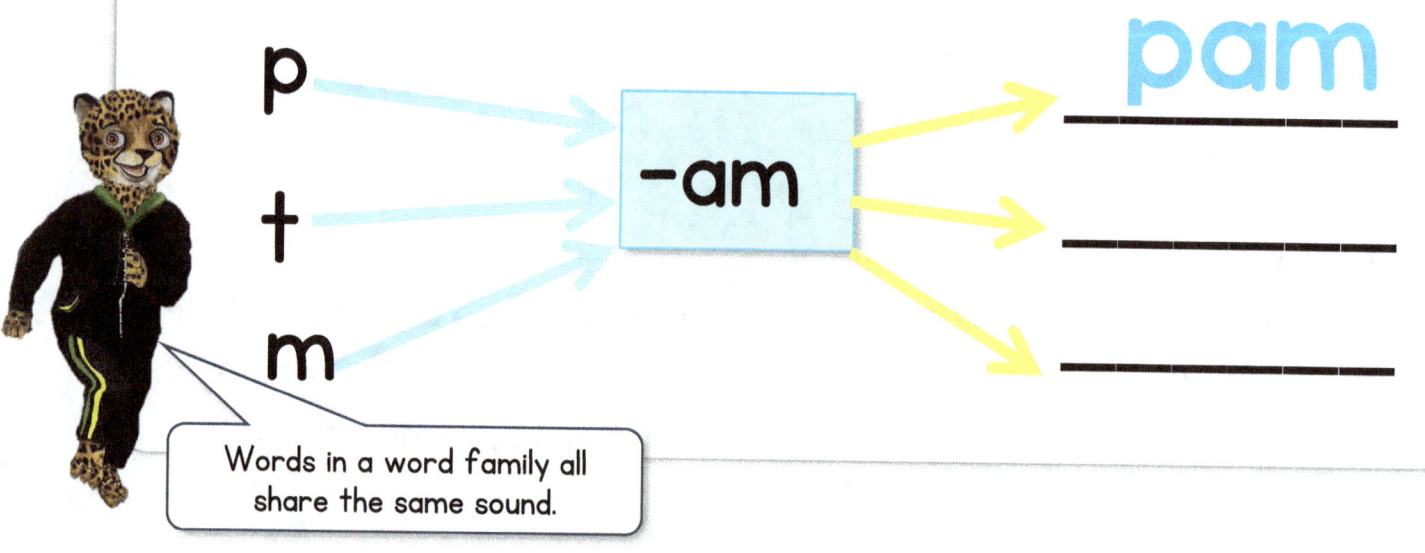

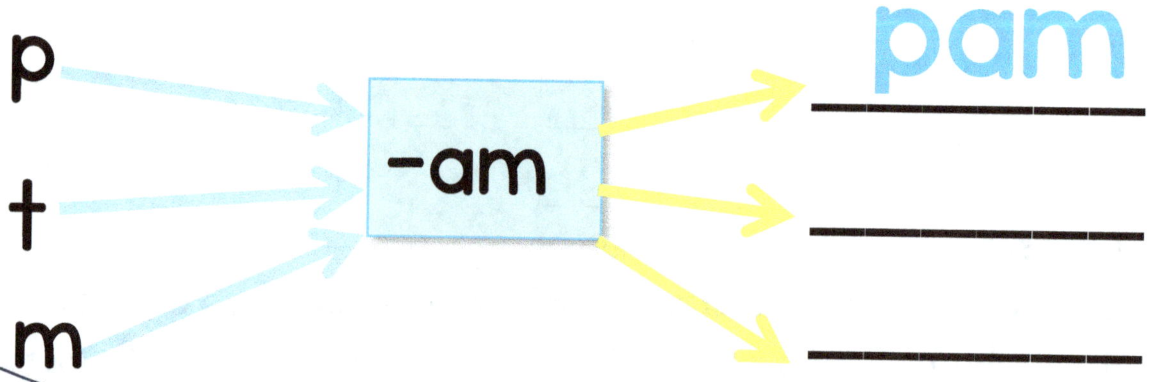

Words in a word family all share the same sound.

Let's take apart

Break each word into sounds. Write the sounds in the boxes.

What sounds can you hear in these words?

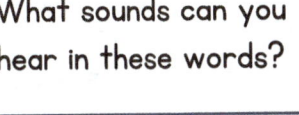

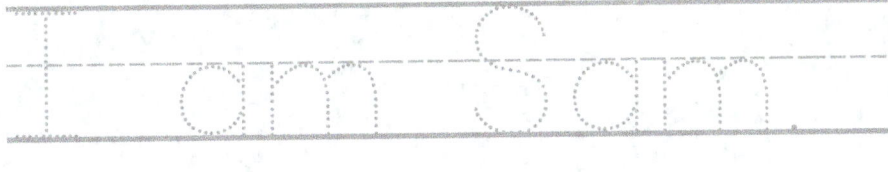

Let's trace

Trace the letters to write sentences.

I am Sam.

It is a tam.

Read the sentences you have written.

Set 2

n, short i, t, r, f

Here are some C-DER books to read:

Sound	C-DER reference	Book title
f	Set 4, Book 32	*My Brother Jim*
n	Set 4, Book 35	*Guess What?*
short i	Set 1, Book 2	*A Day in My Life*
t	Set 3, Book 23	*Off to the Vet*
r	Set 2, Book 15	*Come Back, Pam!*

Let's read together: My Brother Jim

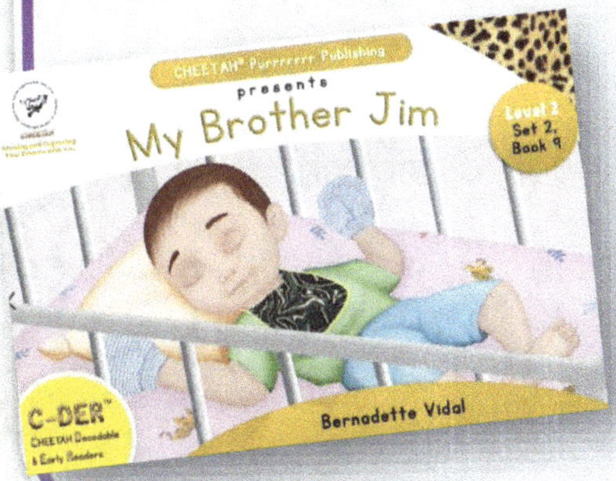
CHEETAH® Purrrrrrr Publishing
presents
My Brother Jim
Level 2 Set 2, Book 9
C-DER
CHEETAH Decodable & Early Readers
Bernadette Vidal

Before you begin, share the title and author of the book, pointing to the front cover. Ask, *"What characters might be in the story?"*

During the story, encourage the child to use the conventions of print by following with their finger as you read (directionality) with a return sweep at the end of each line.

After the story ask, *"What was your favourite part of the book? Why?"*

CHEETAH® train loves a song, zooming as it hums along.
Funny noises came from the sea. Flying fish are flipping free!
Can you guess which sound is next?

Find an instrument, then play and sing along using the lyrics above!
Where do you place your teeth when you make my sound?

F is on the way to town.
CHEETAH® train is slowing down.

Listen as an adult says the words. Draw lines to match each word to the correct picture.

Ff

fly gift leaf

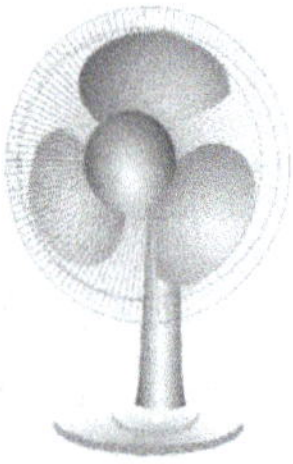

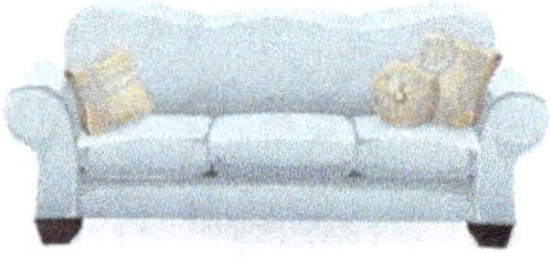

Practise writing the letter *f*.

f f f f f

Listen then <u>underline</u> all the words in the passage with the /f/ sound.

Feri the fox sat on a leaf.

"I can leap far," he said.

"No fox can fly, but all foxes can jump!"

Feri was full of fun.

Colour the face that shows how you feel about the /f/ sound.

Got it! | Almost got it | No, didn't get it

Keep flying high with your learning. The sky is the limit! Come wid me!

Dear Parent: Date: ________________

______________ does/does not fully understand the phonic sound /f/. Please continue to review at home.

Signed: ____________________

Dear Teacher: Date:____________

Thank you. We have reviewed the phonic sound /f/ together. My child had a chance to teach me.

Signed: ____________________

Reward sticker for parent or guardian goes here.

Well done!

____

(write name here)

understands the phonic sound /f/.

Sticker for pupil goes here!

Let's read together: Guess What?

Before you begin, ask, *"Have you ever played 'Guess What?' How do you think you might play it?"*

During the story, stop after every 'Guess What' clue is presented. Ask and discuss *"What could it be?"*

After the story ask, *"Were your 'Guess What' predictions correct? Did you enjoy the game? Why/why not?"*

CHEETAH® train loves a song, zooming as it hums along.
An ant is on Sam's neck, its nest is somewhere on the deck!
Can you guess which sound is next?

Find an instrument, then play and sing along using the lyrics above!
Where is your tongue when you make my sound?

N is on the way to town.
CHEETAH® train is slowing down.

Nn

Say the words. Circle all the pictures that have the /n/ sound.

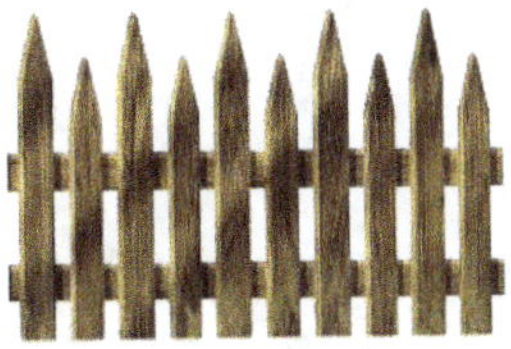

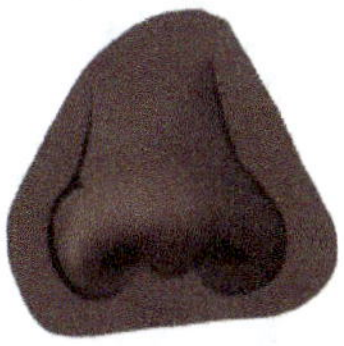

Practise writing the letter *n*.

Listen to the passage, then colour all the words in the passage with the /n/ sound brown.

I am Ned. I nod when I am tired.

At nap time, I snore and snore.

When night comes, it is easy to find me.

I am nicely tucked into my neat bed!

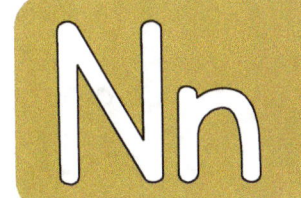

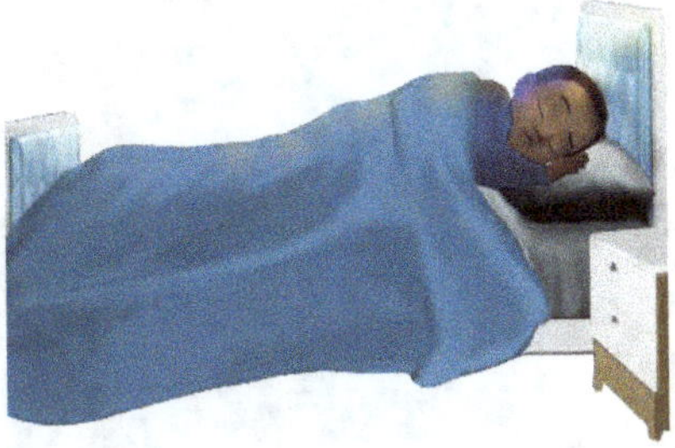

Colour the face that shows how you feel about the /n/ sound.

Got it! | Almost got it | No, didn't get it

Ready for take-off? Let us find out what the next sound is! Come wid mi!

Dear Parent: Date: ________________

_______________ does/does not fully understand the phonic sound /n/. Please continue to review at home.

Signed: ______________________

Dear Teacher: Date:______________

Thank you. We have reviewed the phonic sound /n/ together. My child had a chance to teach me.

Signed: _____________________

Reward sticker for parent or guardian goes here.

Well done!

____

(write name here)

understands the phonic sound /n/.

Sticker for pupil goes here!

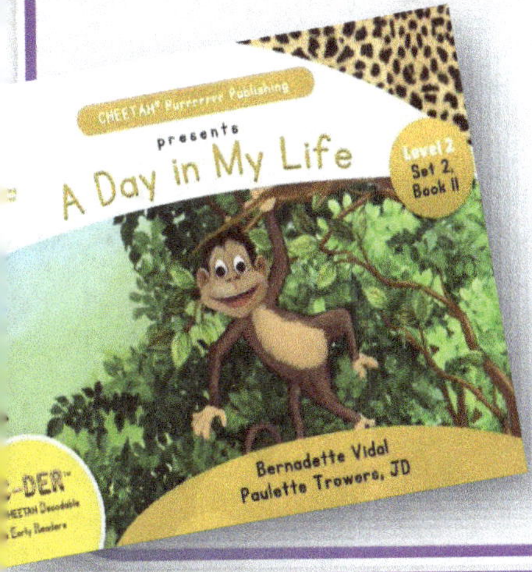

Let's read together: A Day in My Life

Before you begin, ask, "*What clues does the front cover of this book give us about the story?*"

During the story, stop after pages 2, 6, 9, 19 and 28 to ask, "*How do you think the monkey feels? What makes you think this?*"

After the story ask, "*Did the clues on the front cover tell us what this story was about? What else could have been on the front cover?*"

CHEETAH® train plays a song, zooming as it hums along.
Over there a silly pig is itching in a frilly wig.
Can you guess which sound is next?

Find an instrument, then play and sing along using the lyrics above!
Can you make my sound 3 times?

I is on the way to town.
CHEETAH® train is slowing down.

Read the short ĭ words. Draw a picture of each word.

lips

fin

pig

Practise writing the letter *i*.

Listen then underline all the words in the passage with the short ĭ sound.

Jim got a gift. It was two fish.

He put the fish in a jar to swim.

"Big fish, little fish," said Jim.

"Swim, swim, swim and make a wish."

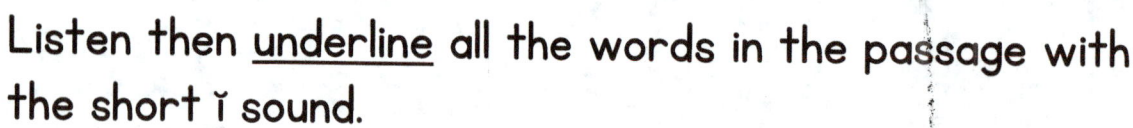

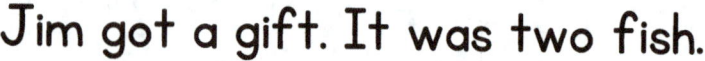

Colour the face that shows how you feel about the short ĭ sound.

Got it! | Almost got it | No, didn't get it

You are learning more and more every day. Keep aiming for the sky! Come wid mi!

Dear Parent: Date: ________________

______________ does/does not fully understand the phonic sound short ĭ. Please continue to review at home.

Signed: _____________________

Dear Teacher: Date:_____________

Thank you. We have reviewed the phonic sound short ĭ together. My child had a chance to teach me.

Signed: ____________________

Reward sticker for parent or guardian goes here.

Well done!

____

(write name here)

understands the phonic sound short ĭ.

Sticker for pupil goes here!

Let's read together: Off to the Vet

Before you begin, ask, *"Do you remember this story? What is the title? What is the book about?"*

During the story, partner read with the child, allowing them to read some pages themselves. Encourage segmentation of unknown words into their constituent phonemes and blending.

After the story, write a sentence telling someone else what the story was about. Use the book to help with correct spelling.

CHEETAH® train loves a song, zooming as it hums along.
Terry loves to eat! Tomatoes are her favourite treat.
Can you guess which sound is next?

Find an instrument, then play and sing along using the lyrics above!
Touch behind your teeth with your tongue!

T is on the way to town.
CHEETAH® train is slowing down.

Tt

Draw lines to guide the animals with the /t/ sound to the tent.

Practise writing the letter *t*.

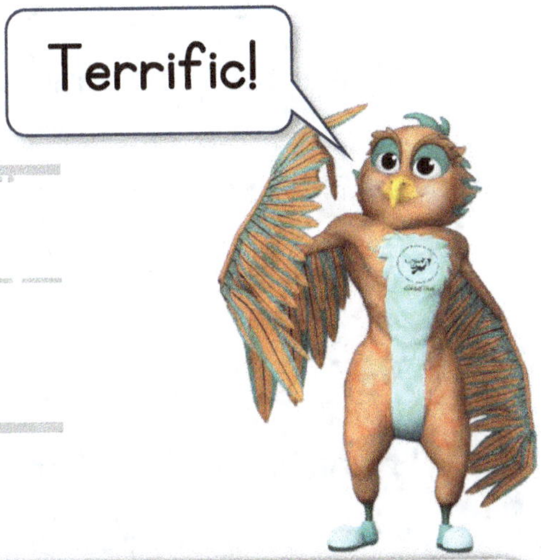

Listen then circle all the words in the passage with the /t/ sound.

Tom has a tiny toy tiger.

He takes it to school every day.

The toy tiger sits on his table.

Tom and his tiger like to tell tales.

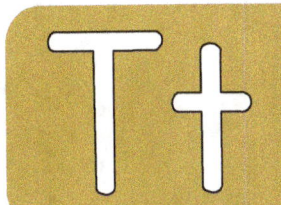

Together we will continue to
learn and discover new things.
Let's keep moving!

Colour the face that shows how you feel about the /t/ sound.

Got it! | Almost got it | No, didn't get it

Dear Parent: Date: _______________

_______________ does/does not fully understand the phonic sound /t/. Please continue to review at home.

Signed: ______________________

Dear Teacher: Date:_____________

Thank you. We have reviewed the phonic sound /t/ together. My child had a chance to teach me.

Signed: ______________________

Reward sticker for parent or guardian goes here.

Well done!

____

(write name here)

understands the phonic sound /t/.

Sticker for pupil goes here!

Let's read together: Come Back, Tam!

Before you begin, ask, "*Can you segment and read the name of the character in the title? What might happen to Tam?*"

During the story, stop after page 1. Ask "*Did you correctly predict the problem? How do you think it might be solved?*" Then later ask, "*What do you think they should do now?*"

After the story ask, "*Did you like the ending? Did you expect that to happen? Why/why not?*"

CHEETAH® train loves a song, zooming as it hums along.
Ryan runs around. The train is rumbling on the ground.
Can you guess which sound is next?

Find an instrument, then play and sing along using the lyrics above!
Practise my sound while you look in a mirror!

R is on the way to town.
CHEETAH® train is slowing down.

Rr

Say the words. Tick (✓) the pictures that contain the /r/ sound.

☐  ☐ 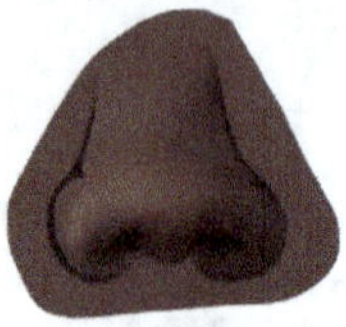 ☐ 

☐  ☐ 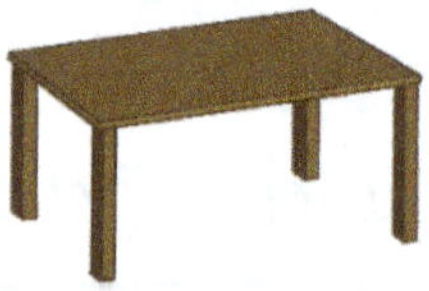 ☐ 

Practise writing the letter *r*.

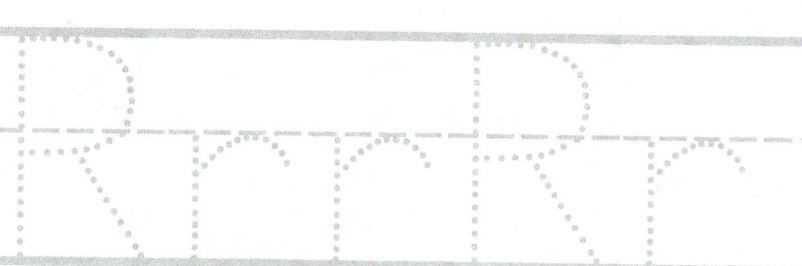

Listen then colour all the words in the passage with the /r/ sound red.

Roy, the red rabbit, loves to run.

After the rain, he races in the roaring river.

His fur gets wet, but Roy doesn't care.

He just loves to run around and race.

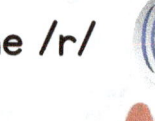

Colour the face that shows how you feel about the /r/ sound.

Got it! | Almost got it | No, didn't get it

If you are not sure about a sound, ask a friend or an adult for help.

Dear Parent: Date: _______________

______________ does/does not fully understand the phonic sound /r/. Please continue to review at home.

Signed: _____________________

Dear Teacher: Date:_____________

Thank you. We have reviewed the phonic sound /r/ together. My child had a chance to teach me.

Signed: ____________________

Reward sticker for parent or guardian goes here.

Well done!

____

(write name here)

understands the phonic sound /r/.

Sticker for pupil goes here!

CHEETAH's review

Use the letters representing the missing sounds to complete the words.

f	n	i	t	r

_ i s h

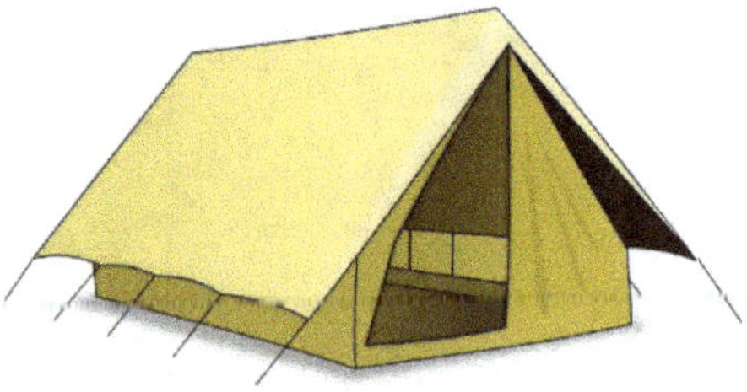

t e _ t

_a t

p e _

c a _

CHEETAH's review

Use the letters to make as many short words as you can.

p a s

f r

n i t

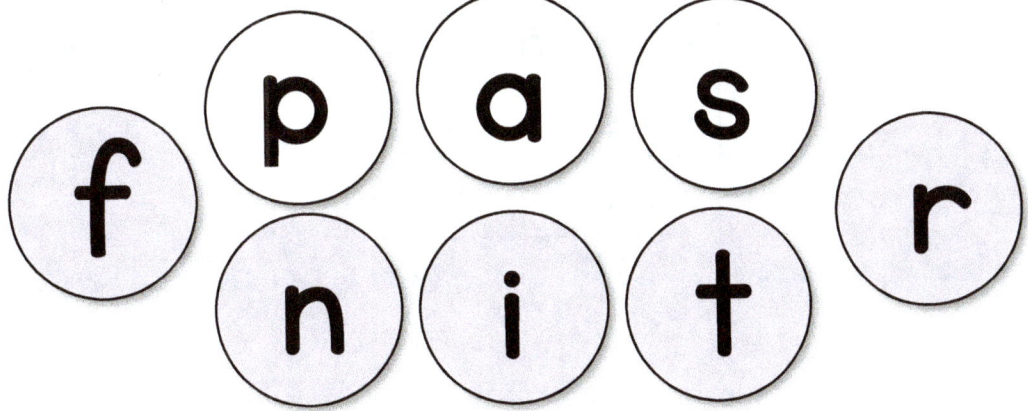

How many words did you make? Teach someone at home how to create words using letters.

CHEETAH®'s review

Find the high frequency words in the wordsearch.

b	i	g	r	m
f	n	d	u	g
o	g	a	n	d
u	e	s	a	f
r	t	f	l	y

and big fly run get four

Play the game *I spy with my little eye* using the /f/, /n/, short i, /t/ and /r/ sounds.

Solve the clues to complete the crossword.

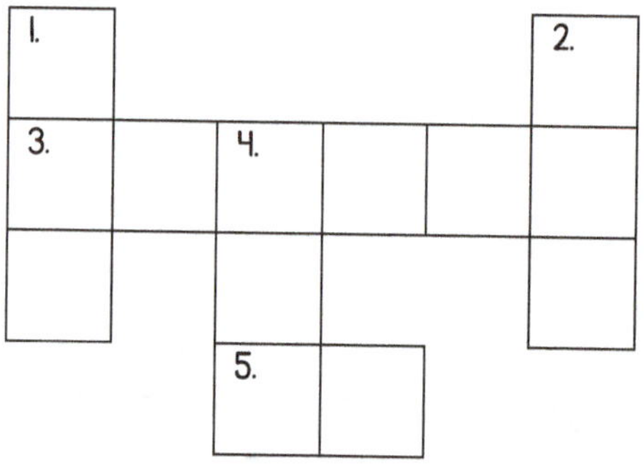

Across:

3. Another word for small.
5. The boy is sitting __ the chair.

Down:

1. An insect with wings.
2. The colour of a tomato.
4. One and one makes this number.

CHEETAH® Purrrrrr Publishing

presents

Pet on the Mat

Sets 1 & 2

Set I: s. short a, m, short e, p · Set 2: f, n, short i, t, r

1

Sam met Pam on the mat.

2

Pam sat on the mat with Sam.

3

Pam sat on the mat with Sam.

4

The pet sat on the mat by Sam.

5

Have a sip, Pam.

6

Can the pet sip it?

The pet can tip it!

Nip the mat!

Rip!

The pet gave Pam the tin.

The pet had a nap on the mat by Pam and Sam.

Let's create words

Complete the table. Put the letters together to make words.

beginning sound	middle sound	end sound	words created
f n t r	i	t	fit, nit, tit, rit, fig, nig
		g	
		p	
		n	
		m	

List the words that you do not know the meaning of.

____

____

Ask an adult what they mean.

Sound out the words you have made.

Let's put together

Connect the boxes to make words from the -at word family. Write them in the given space.

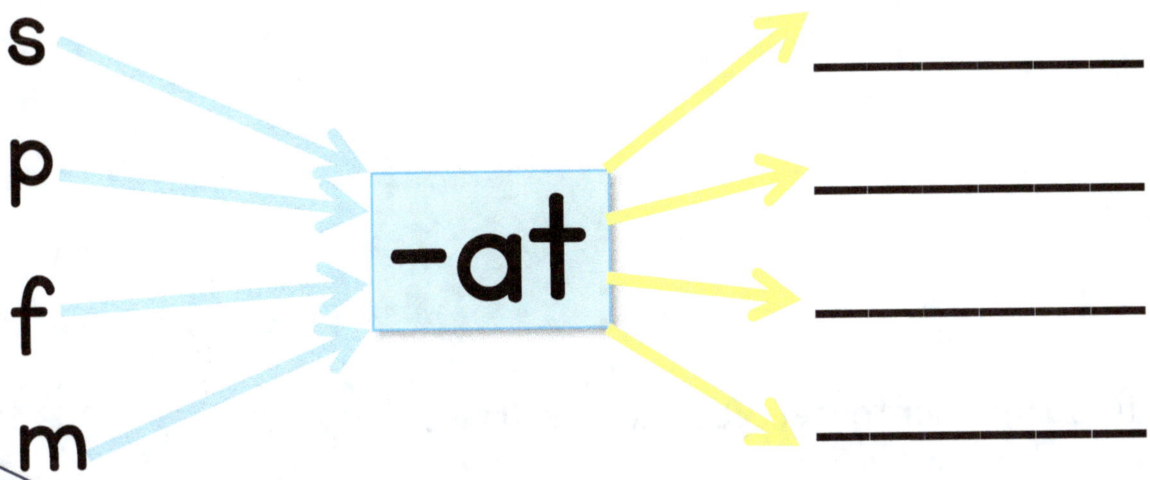
s
p
f
m
-at

Knowing word families will make it easier to read and

Let's take apart

Break each word into sounds. Write the sounds in the boxes.

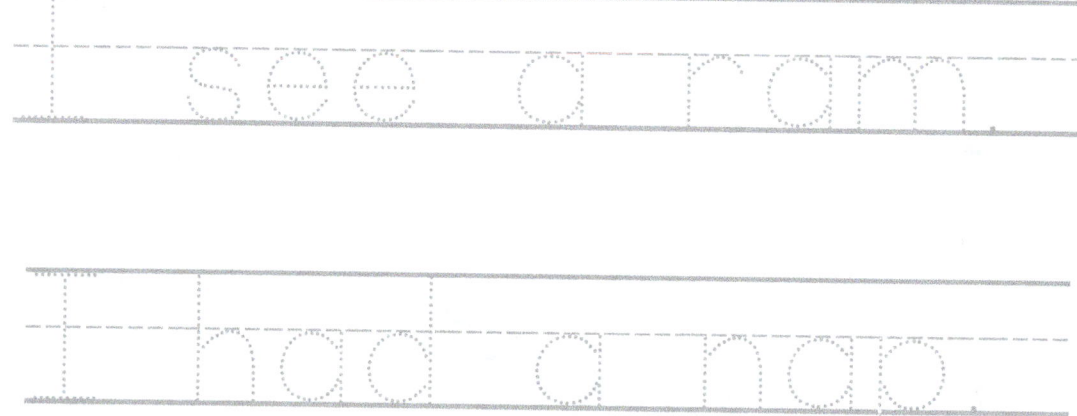

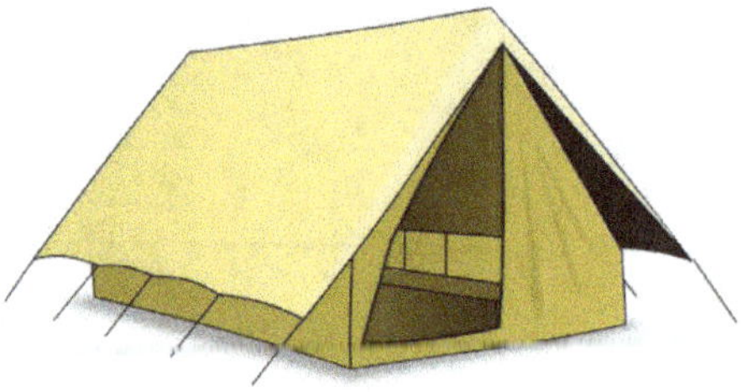

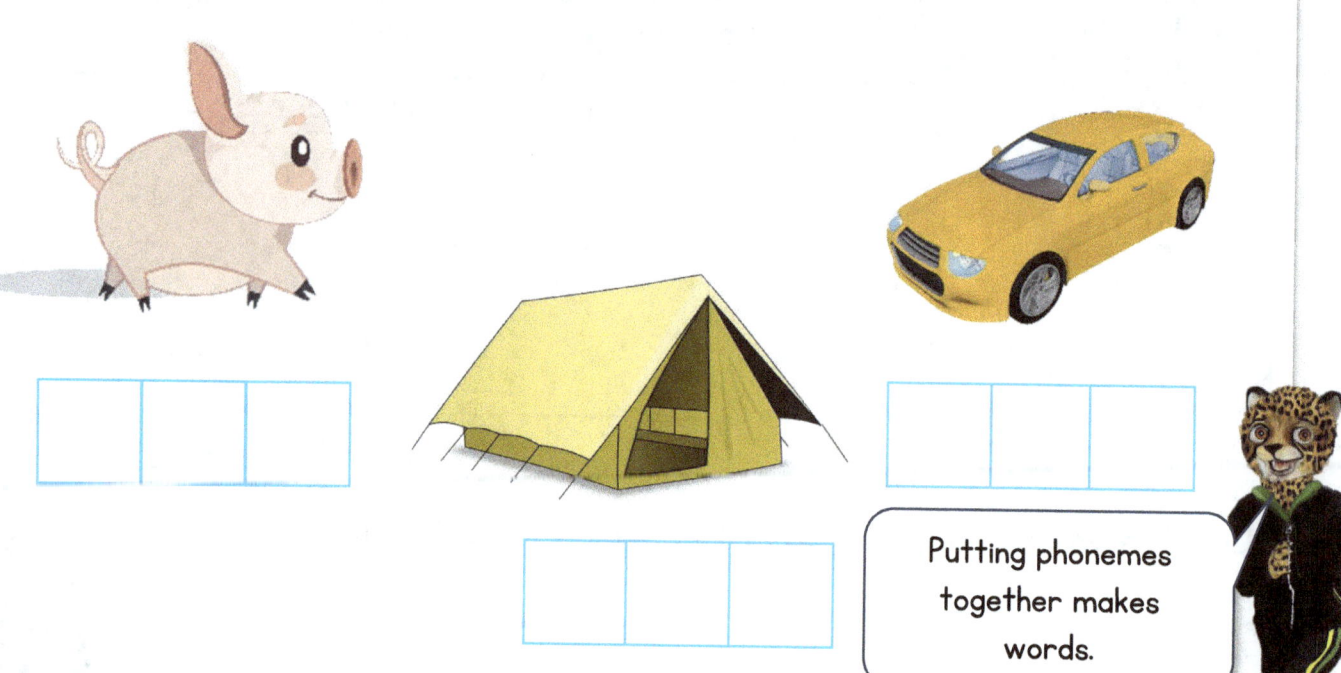

Putting phonemes together makes words.

Let's trace

Trace the letters to write sentences.

I see a ram.

I had a nap.

Read the sentences you have written.

CHEETAH® reward stickers

MARVELOUS!
SPECTACULAR!
YOU NAILED IT!
SHINE ON!
YOU NAILED IT!
BRILLIANT EFFORT!
YOU DID IT!
GREAT!
GREAT TRY!

KEEP TRYING!

Did you have fun? I did!

This page has been left blank so you can cut out the reward stickers.

Set 3

/d/, short ŏ, hard /g/, /h/ and /k/.

Here are some C-DER books to read:

Sound	C-DER reference	Book title
/d/	Set 3, Book 26	*Ted Disobeys*
short o	Set 3, Book 20	*Look What I Got*
hard g	Set 5, Book 40	*Glenda Needs Help*
/h/	Set 7, Book 55	*Hilda and her Chicks*
/k/	Set 7, Book 60	*At the Kite Festival*

5+

Let's read together: Ted Disobeys

Before you begin, explain the meaning of "disobeys". Ask, "*Have you ever disobeyed? What happened?*"

During the story, stop after page 6. Ask, "*How did Ted disobey? How do you think Ted feels? What might happen next?*"

After the story ask, "*What did you think of the ending? Is that what you predicted would happen? What did Ted learn?*"

CHEETAH® train loves a song, zooming as it hums along.
Daisy loves a dancing beat, drumming music on her seat.
Can you guess which sound is next?

Find an instrument, then play and sing along using the lyrics above!
Touch your throat as you make my sound. Can you feel the vibration?

D is on the way to town.
CHEETAH® train is slowing down.

Dd

Draw a line from the pictures with a /d/ sound to the letter *d*.

Dd

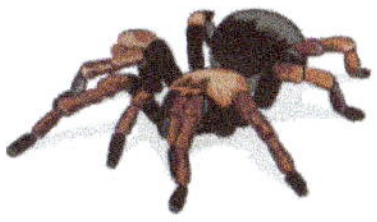

Practise writing the letter *d*.

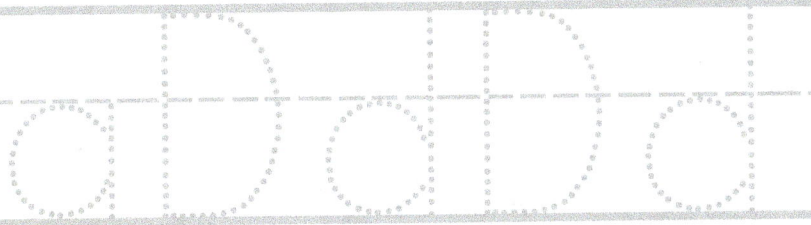

You can do this!

Listen then colour all the words in the passage with the /d/ sound red.

Ted had a big red bed.

He would jump on it until he was fed.

His mum said, "Off to bed, Ted!"

Ted climbed into bed, resting his head.

Colour the face that shows how you feel about the /d/ sound.

Got it! | Almost got it | No, didn't get it

I am impressed by how much you are learning! Come fly with me to the next sound.

Dear Parent: Date: ________________

______________ does/does not fully understand the phonic sound /d/. Please continue to review at home.

Signed: ____________________

Dear Teacher: Date:______________

Thank you. We have reviewed the phonic sound /d/ together. My child had a chance to teach me.

Signed: ____________________

Reward sticker for parent or guardian goes here.

You did it!

____

(write name here)

understands the phonic sound /d/.

Sticker for pupil goes here!

Let's read together: Look What I Got

Before you begin ask, "*What is the title of this story? What do you think it will be about?*"

During the story, after each gift is announced, stop to ask, "*What could Ben do with this gift?*"

After the story ask, "*What gifts did Ben receive? Which was his favourite? Why did he love it so much?*"

CHEETAH® train loves a song, zooming as it hums along.
An ox is on a box! He is dancing in his orange socks.
Can you guess which sound is next?

Find an instrument, then play and sing along using the lyrics above!
Can you say my sound three times?

O is on the way to town.
CHEETAH® train is slowing down.

Oo

Say the words. Circle the word that matches the picture.

pot

not

ox

on

rock

lock

box

fox

Practise writing the letter ŏ.

Listen and circle all the words in the passage with the short ŏ sound.

Bob the dog got a job in a shop.

The shop had lots of socks and tops.

On his day off, he shot out of bed.

"I am off to have some fun!" said Bob.

Colour the face that shows how you feel about the short ŏ sound.

Got it!
Almost got it
No, didn't get it

Be proud of yourself for spreading your wings!

Dear Parent: Date: _______________

_______________ does/does not fully understand the phonic sound short ŏ. Please continue to review at home.

Signed: ______________________

Dear Teacher: Date: ______________

Thank you. We have reviewed the phonic sound short ŏ together. My child had a chance to teach me.

Signed: ______________________

Reward sticker for parent or guardian goes here.

Good work!

____

(write name here)

understands the phonic sound short ŏ.

Sticker for pupil goes here!

<u>Let's read together: Glenda Needs Help</u>

Before you begin ask, "*Where might this story be set? What makes you think that? What might the story be about?*"

During the story, stop after each page and read the rhyming words together. E.g. *Ben, pen, hen.*

After the story, look back at the rhyming word groups. Ask, "*What is the same about these words? What is different?*"

CHEETAH® train loves a song, zooming as it hums along.
A goat is eating grass, grinning as the train goes past.
Can you guess which sound is next?

Find an instrument, then play and sing along using the lyrics above!
Where is your tongue as you make my sound?

G is on the way to town.
CHEETAH® train is slowing down.

Gg

Put a cross (X) through the pictures that do **not** have the hard /g/ sound.

Practise writing the letter *g*.

<u>Underline</u> all the words in the passage with the hard /g/ sound.

Gabby the goat loves to gallop.

She goes around the garden,

gobbling up the green grass.

Goodness, Gabby is a greedy goat!

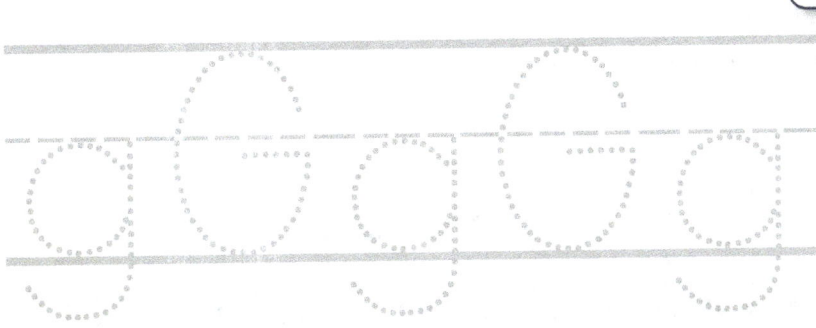

Colour the face that shows how you feel about the hard /g/ sound.

Got it! | Almost got it | No, didn't get it

We learn from the mistakes we make. Let us keep flying through phonics!

Dear Parent: Date: ________________

_______________ does/does not fully understand the phonic sound hard /g/. Please continue to review at home.

Signed: ______________________

Dear Teacher: Date:_____________

Thank you. We have reviewed the phonic sound hard /g/ together. My child had a chance to teach me.

Signed: _____________________

Reward sticker for parent or guardian goes here.

Well done!

____

(write name here)

understands the phonic sound hard /g/.

Sticker for pupil goes here!

CHEETAH® Purrrrrrr Publishing
presents
Hilda and Her Chicks
Level 2
Set 3,
Book 24
Bernadette Vidal
Paulette Trowers, JD
C-DER

Let's read together: Hilda and her Chicks

Before you begin, ask, "*Who do you think Hilda is? Why do you think this? Could Hilda be someone else?*"

During the story, stop after page 1 to ask, "*Is Hilda who you thought she would be? Which words tell you who she is?*"

After the story ask, "*What can you tell me about the character of Hilda? Which part of the story told you that?*"

CHEETAH® train loves a song, zooming as it hums along.
There is Hilda on her horse! She is happy as she rides the course.
Can you guess which sound is next?

Find an instrument, then play and sing along using the lyrics above!
Hold your hand before your mouth as you make my sound. What do you notice?

H is on the way to town.
CHEETAH® train is slowing down.

Hh

Colour the things that begin with the letter *h*.

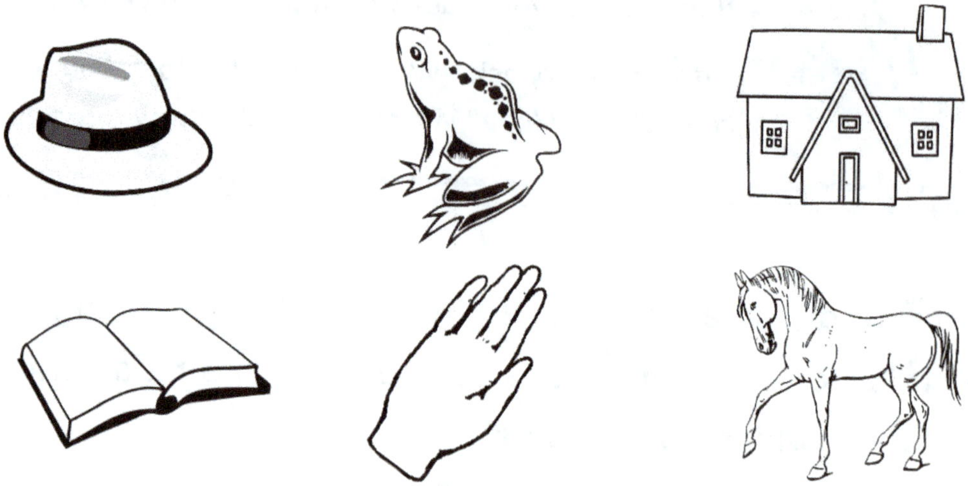

Practise writing the letter *h*.

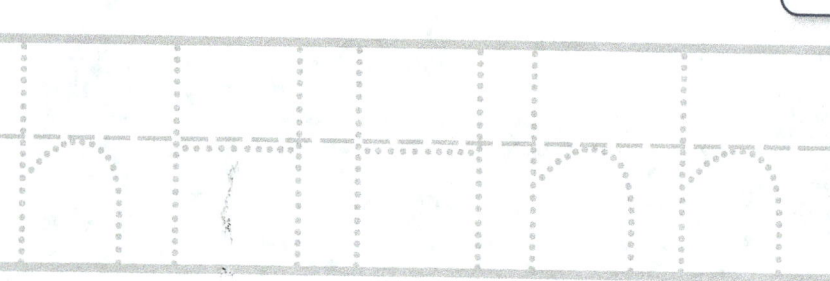

Listen and <u>underline</u> all the words in the passage with the /h/ sound.

Henry the horse lived on a hill.

He had a hobby of hopping high.

"Will today be a happy day of hopping?"

He would ask himself each day as he hopped.

Colour the face that shows how you feel about the /h/ sound.

Got it! | Almost got it | No, didn't get it

Together we will continue to learn and discover new things. Let's keep moving!

Dear Parent: Date: ________________

_______________ does/does not fully understand the phonic sound /h/. Please continue to review at home.

Signed: ______________________

Dear Teacher: Date: ______________

Thank you. We have reviewed the phonic sound /h/ together. My child had a chance to teach me.

Signed: ____________________

Reward sticker for parent or guardian goes here.

Congratulations!

Sticker for pupil goes here!

____

(write name here)

understands the phonic sound /h/.

<u>Let's read together: At the Kite Festival</u>

Before you begin ask, "*Are you excited to read this story? Why/why not? Have you ever seen a kite fly?*"

During the story, stop on page 15. Ask, "*Can you read this page with me?*" Encourage identification of sounds and blending.

After the story ask, "*What happened at the beginning/ middle/ end of this story? Can you show/read me this part in the book?*"

CHEETAH® train loves a song, zooming as it hums along.
A crab is kicking balls, clacking with its clicking claws.
Can you guess which sound is next?

Find an instrument, then play and sing along using the lyrics above!
Feel the air from our mouth as you say our sound.

CK is on the way to town.
CHEETAH® train is slowing down.

Cc Kk

Use a *c* or *k* to complete each word.

_an

bi_e

wal_

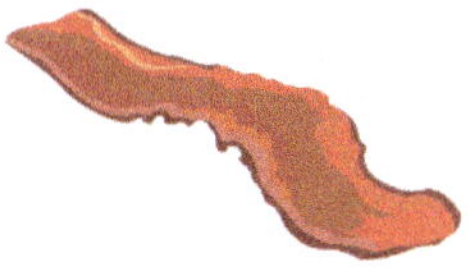

ba_on

Practise writing the letter *c* and *k*.

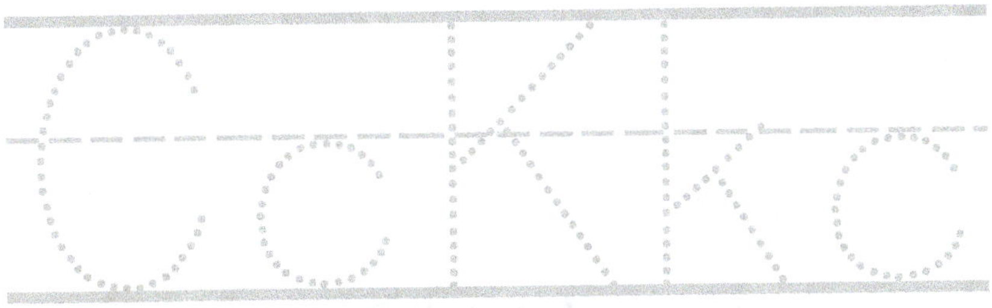

Listen and circle all the words in the passage with the /k/ sound.

"Let us make a picnic" Katie called to Caleb.

They put cupcakes, kiwis, and coconut water into a bag.

Next, the children biked to the park.

They sat on a rock and ate their picnic snacks.

Colour the face that shows how you feel about the /k/ sound.

Got it! | Almost got it | No, didn't get it

I am proud of your hard work this week! Let us glide to CHEETAH's review..

Dear Parent: Date: ________________

_______________ does/does not fully understand the phonic sound /k/. Please continue to review at home.

Signed: ______________________

Dear Teacher: Date: ______________

Thank you. We have reviewed the phonic sound /k/ together. My child had a chance to teach me.

Signed: _____________________

Reward sticker for parent or guardian goes here.

Wonderful!

____

(write name here)

understands the phonic sound /k/.

Sticker for pupil goes here!

CHEETAH®'s review

Look at each row. Circle the picture that has the sound at the beginning, middle or end of the word.

d	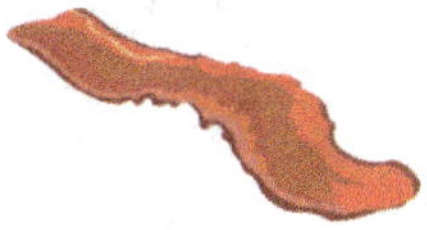		
short o	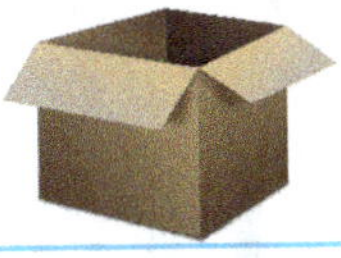		
hard g			
h			
hard c or k			

Find the high frequency words in the wordsearch.

s	t	o	p	c
d	h	e	l	p
o	a	w	i	m
w	n	c	a	n
n	k	e	t	f

stop down good help thank can

CHEETAH®'s review

Use the letters to make as many words as you can.

Circle all the words you make with the short ŏ sound.

d	g	h
n	o	c
e	k	t

Solve the clues to complete the crossword.

Word bank

dig
stop
kite
head
help

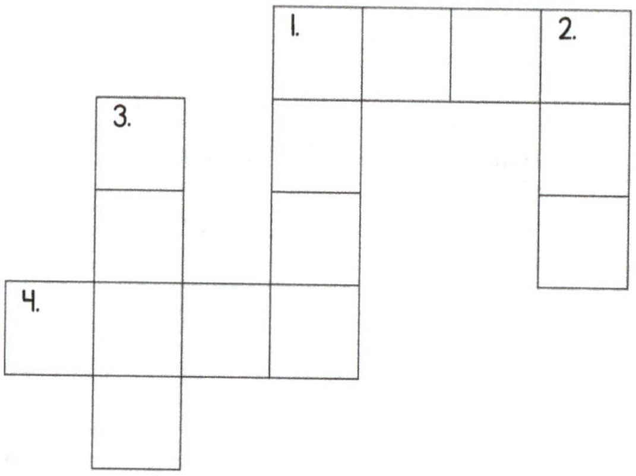

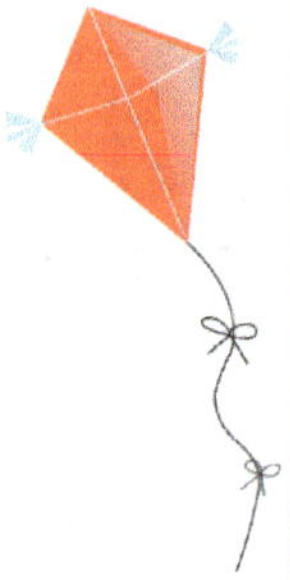

Across:

1. The part of your body with eyes, ears, a mouth and a nose.
4. Cars must do this when a traffic light is red.

Down:

1. If you have a problem, you ask for this.
2. You do this with a spade to make a hole.
3. A toy you can fly in a windy day.

Where Is the Sock?

d, short o, g, h, c/k

A CHEETAH® Poster Story

Mick and Nat sit on the dock.
The cat is by the dock.
1
"Get your sock, Mick!"
2
"Is the sock in the sack, Mick?"
3
"It is not here, Nat."
4
"Where is a cop, Mick?"
Nat and Mick go to get a cop.
5
The cop, Mick, and Nap hop to the dock.
6

Set 3

Where Is the Sock?

d, short o, g, h, c/k

A CHEETAH® Poster Story

"There it is! By the big red rock."
7

Nat and Mick kick the red rock.
8

"Kid, is that your cat?"
9

"Look! The cat had the sock!"
said Mick and Nat.
10

She is a top cop!
11

Let's create

Complete the table. Put the letters together to make words.

beginning sound	middle sound	end sound	words created
d g h c	o	t	dot, got, hot, cot
		g	
		p	
		k	
		w	

Use a different colour pencil crayon to draw circles around the words you do not know. Ask an adult what they mean.

Let's put together

Connect the boxes to make words from the -op word family. Write them in the given space.

h
m
p
t
_op

Can you hear that the words in a word family all rhyme?

Let's take apart

Break each word into sounds. Write the sounds in the boxes.

Recognising phonemes will help you to read new words.

Let's trace

Trace the letters to write sentences.

It is not hot.

A dog bit me!

Read the sentences you have written.

CHEETAH® reward stickers

MARVELOUS!

SPECTACULAR!

YOU NAILED IT!

SHINE ON!

YOU NAILED IT!

BRILLIANT EFFORT!

YOU DID IT!

GREAT!

GREAT TRY!

KEEP TRYING!

Did you have fun? I did!

This page has been left blank so you can cut out the reward stickers.

Set 4

/l/, /b/, short ŭ, soft /g/ and long ā.

Here are some C-DER books to read:

Sound	C-DER reference	Book title
/l/	Set 1, Book 7	*In the Sky*
/b/	Set 1, Book 1	*Meet My Family*
short ŭ	Set 2, Book 16	*A Bug on the Rug*
long ā	Set 2, Book 13	*The Big Race*

Let's read together: In the Sky

Before you begin ask, "*What do you think this story might be about? What other things might we see in this story?*"

During the story, stop when the helicopter and the aeroplane appear. Ask, "*Is this one of the things you expected to see? How did you know it might appear in the story?*"

After the story ask, "*Do you think this story could have really happened? Why/why not?*"

CHEETAH® train loves a song, zooming as it hums along.
It whizzes through the land! Look! There's Lily in the sand.
Can you guess which sound is next?

Find an instrument, then play and sing along using the lyrics above!
Flick your tongue to make my sound!

L is on the way to town.
CHEETAH® train is slowing down.

Say the words and look at the pictures. Circle the correct word.

Ll

fall

ball

leg

lid

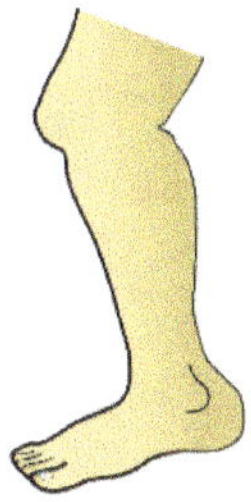

old

belt

Practise writing the letter *l*.

Listen then underline all the words in the passage with the /l/ sound.

Lola the ladybug loved to fly from leaf to leaf.

She lived on a large, green plant.

Lola liked to look at the world from high above.

Life was always lively for Lola.

Colour the face that shows how you feel about the /l/ sound.

Got it! | Almost got it | No, didn't get it

Spead your wings and we will fly to the next sound!

Dear Parent: Date: ________________

_______________ does/does not fully understand the phonic sound /l/. Please continue to review at home.

Signed: ______________________

Dear Teacher: Date:_____________

Thank you. We have reviewed the phonic sound /l/ together. My child had a chance to teach me.

Signed: _____________________

Reward sticker for parent or guardian goes here.

Excellent!

____

(write name)

understands the phonic sound /l/.

Sticker for pupil goes here!

CHEETAH® Purrrrrr Publishing
presents
Going fishing
Level 2
Set 2,
Book 14
Bernadette Vidal
Paulette Trowers, JD
C-DER

Let's read together: Going Fishing

Before you begin ask, "*Who do you think the characters will be in the story? Where do you think it will be set?*"

During the story, read page 4 together. Reinforce the conventions of print (directionality and return sweep).

After the story ask, "*Would you like to go fishing? Who would you choose to go with?*"

CHEETAH® train loves a song, zooming as it hums along.
It speeds by in a rush! Look! There's Bobby with his bus.
Can you guess which sound is next?

Find an instrument, then play and sing along using the lyrics above!
Use your lips to make my sound!
B b

B is on the way to town.
CHEETAH® train is slowing down.

Bb

Listen as an adult reads the words. Tick to show if the /b/ sound is at the start, middle or end of the word.

☐ start
☐ middle
☐ end

☐ start
☐ middle
☐ end

☐ start
☐ middle
☐ end

☐ start
☐ middle
☐ end

Practise writing the letter *b*.

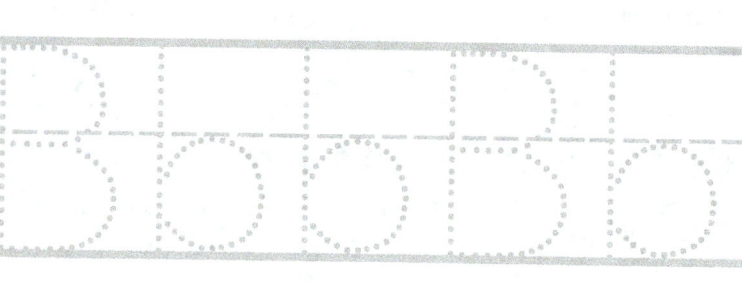

Listen then <u>underline</u> all the words in the passage with the /b/ sound.

Billy had a book about a brave bear.

He would read it before bed every night.

"Bears are so big and brave," Billy would say.

Billy wanted to be as brave as the bear.

Colour the face that shows how you feel about the /b/ sound.

Got it! | Almost got it | No, didn't get it

Remember, even owls have to learn before they can fly.

Dear Parent: Date: ________________

_______________ does/does not fully understand the phonic sound /b/. Please continue to review at home.

Signed: ______________________

Dear Teacher: Date:______________

Thank you. We have reviewed the phonic sound /b/ together. My child had a chance to teach me.

Signed: _____________________

Reward sticker for parent or guardian goes here.

Brilliant!

____

(write name

understands the phonic sound /b/.

Sticker for pupil goes here!

CHEETAH® Purrrrrrr Publishing
presents
A Bug On the Rug
Level 2
Set 4,
Book 34
C-DER™
Bernadette Vidal
Paulette Trowers, JD

Let's read together: A Bug on the Rug

Before you begin, introduce the short ŭ sound. Ask, *"Can you blend the phonemes to read the words in the title of this book?"*

During the story, stop after reading page 2. Ask, *"How would you feel if there was a bug on the rug? What would you do?"*

After the story ask, *"How did Bella help the bug? What might have happened if she had not been there?"*

CHEETAH® train loves a song, zooming as it hums along.
It rushes up the hill, where bunny sits so calm and still.
Can you guess which sound is next?

Find an instrument, then play and sing along using the lyrics above!
What shape is your mouth when you make my sound?

U is on the way to town.
CHEETAH® train is slowing down.

Uu

Draw lines to match the short ŭ words to the pictures.

sun bus bug cup

Practise writing the letter *u*.

Listen then <u>underline</u> all the words in the passage with the short ŭ sound.

A funny pup named Bud loved to run.

He would run up the hill and then run down.

"Bud, you run so much!" his mum would say.

But Bud found it so fun to run under the sun.

Colour the face that shows how you feel about the short ŭ sound.

Got it!

Almost got it

No, didn't get it

The sky is the limit! Let us keep going together.

Dear Parent: Date: ________________

_______________ does/does not fully understand the phonic sound short ŭ. Please continue to review at home.

Signed: ______________________

Dear Teacher: Date:______________

Thank you. We have reviewed the phonic sound short ŭ together. My child had a chance to teach me.

Signed: _____________________

Reward sticker for parent or guardian goes here.

Super effort!

____

(write name)

understands the phonic sound short ŭ.

Sticker for pupil goes here!

Let's read together: At the Zoo

Before you begin ask, "*What animals might the characters see at the zoo?*" List the suggestions made.

During the story, stop after each animal appears. Refer back to the list, and tick beside the animal if it was predicted.

After the story ask, "*How many animals did you predict correctly? Were there any animals you didn't expect to see?*"

CHEETAH® train loves a song, zooming as it hums along.
Gentle Geoff loves the train, riding home with his friend Jane.
Can you guess which sound is next?

Find an instrument, then play and sing along using the lyrics above!
Can you make my sound 3 times?

G is on the way to town.
CHEETAH® train is slowing down.

Gg

Say the words. Circle the words with the soft /g/ sound.

Practise writing the letter /g/.

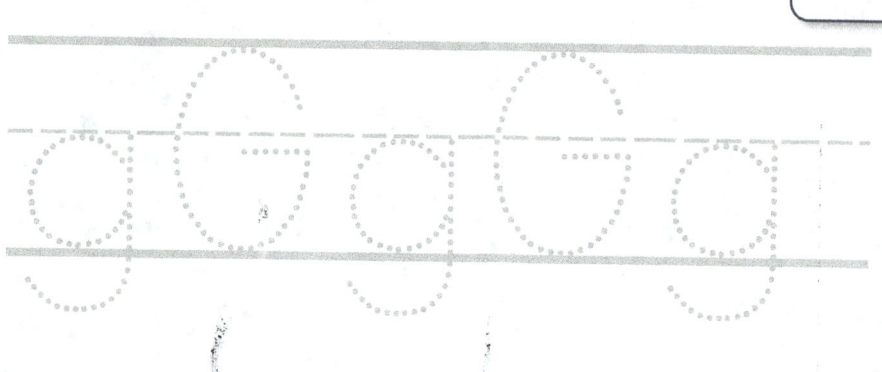

Listen then underline all the words in the passage with the soft /g/ sound.

At school, Gina loved to learn.

She learned about giant mountains and great oceans.

"Do you know about giraffes?" her friend Roger asked.

"Yes! They are gentle and tall, with a giant neck!"

Colour the face that shows how you feel about the soft /g/ sound.

Got it! | Almost got it | No, didn't get it

Believe in yourself and you will fly high!

Dear Parent: Date: ________________

______________ does/does not fully understand the phonic sound soft /g/. Please continue to review at home.

Signed: _____________________

Dear Teacher: Date: ______________

Thank you. We have reviewed the phonic sound soft /g/ together. My child had a chance to teach me.

Signed: ____________________

Reward sticker for parent or guardian goes here.

Great job!

____

(write name

understands the phonic sound soft /g/.

Sticker for pupil goes here!

Let's read together: The Big Race

Before you begin, explain that this story is about Usain Bolt. Ask, *"Can you tell me anything about who Usain Bolt is?"*

During the story, encourage the child to read along, assisting with words they may not have seen before.

After the story ask, *"Can you use the pictures in the book to tell me what happened at the beginning, middle and end of this story?"*

CHEETAH® train loves a song, zooming as it hums along.
It zooms across the land, past elephants and yellow sand.
Can you guess which sound is next?

Find an instrument, then play and sing along using the lyrics above!
Move your jaw to make my sound!

A is on the way to town.
CHEETAH® train is slowing down.

Aa ay a_e ai

Look at the pictures. Use *a* or *ay* to complete each word.

__ngel

tr__

__pron

pl__

Practise writing the letter *a* and *e*.

a e a e a

When I see 2 vowel friends, the first one always leads by saying its own name.

Listen then <u>underline</u> all the words in the passage with the long ā sound.

"May, your cake is amazing!" said Jay.

May had baked a cake that day.

"Thank you, Jay," said May.

"I found out how to bake from watching a play."

Colour the face that shows how you feel about the long ā sound.

Got it! | Almost got it | No, didn't get it

You have spread your wings and learnt so much!

Dear Parent: Date: ________________

______________ does/does not fully understand the phonic sound long ā. Please continue to review at home.

Signed: ____________________

Dear Teacher: Date:____________

Thank you. We have reviewed the phonic sound long ā sound together. My child had a chance to teach me.

Signed: ____________________

Reward sticker for parent or guardian goes here.

Amazing!

____

(write name

understands the phonic sound long ā.

Sticker for pupil goes here!

CHEETAH's review

Use the picture and the words to write a sentence. Don't forget to start with a capital letter and end with a period.

sun is
big The

is blue
rug The

baby at
Look the

Run the
bus to

Use the letters to make as many short ŭ and long ā words as you can. Letters can be used more than once, and nonsense words are welcome. Be creative and have fun!

n r y u a i e g l b

CHEETAH's review

Find the high frequency words in the wordsearch.

b	u	t	p	s
l	u	m	d	a
u	p	l	a	y
e	o	e	t	r
i	n	t	e	n

blue   but   say   play   upon   let   ate

Use the pictures to complete the crossword.

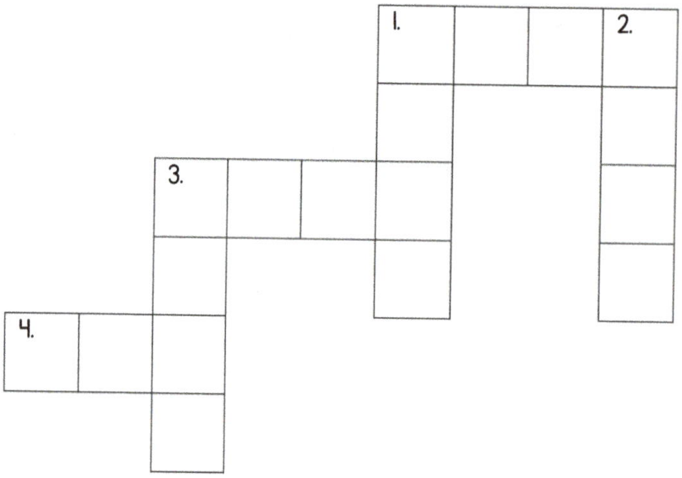

Across:

1. 

3. 

4. 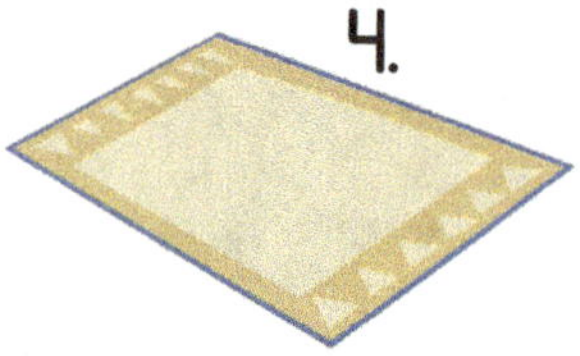

Down:

1. 

2. 

3. 

Make a Game

A CHEETAH® Poster Story

l, b, u, (soft) g, a (a-e)

Gus was late to see Ben at the lake!

Ben and Gus had the same cape!

Gus and Ben sat on a log in the sun.

Ben made a cake. He gave some cake to Gus.

The cat came to see Ben.

The cat had a name tag with a gem. The name was Cal.

Make a Game

Set 4

l, b, u, (soft) g, a (a-e)

Cal gave the back of the cape a tug.
7

Gus gave his cape to Cal.
8

Cal, Ben, and Gus made a fun game.
9

Gus made base one with tape.
10

Ben made base two by the lake.
11

Gus ran to the base with Cal.
12

"Good game, Gus and Cal!" said Ben.
13

Let's create

Complete the table. Put the letters together to make words.

beginning sound	middle sound	end sound	words created
l		t	
b	u	g	
	a	m	
g		n	

List the words that you do not know the meaning of.

____

____

Ask an adult what they mean.

Sound out the words you have made.

Let's put together

Connect the boxes to make words from the -op word family. Write them in the given space.

m
h
p
b
_ay

____

____

____

____

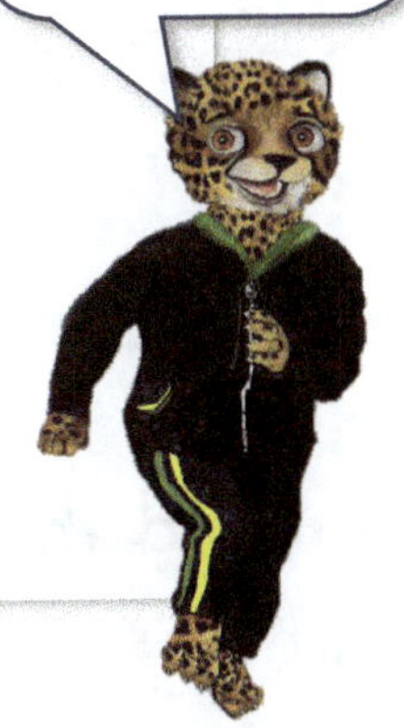
This word family shares the long a sound.

Let's take apart

Break each word into sounds. Write the sounds in the boxes.

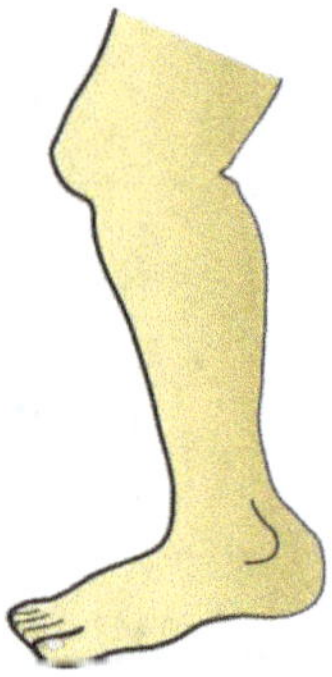

Count how many phonemes each word has.

Let's trace

Trace the letters to write sentences.

I am on the bus.

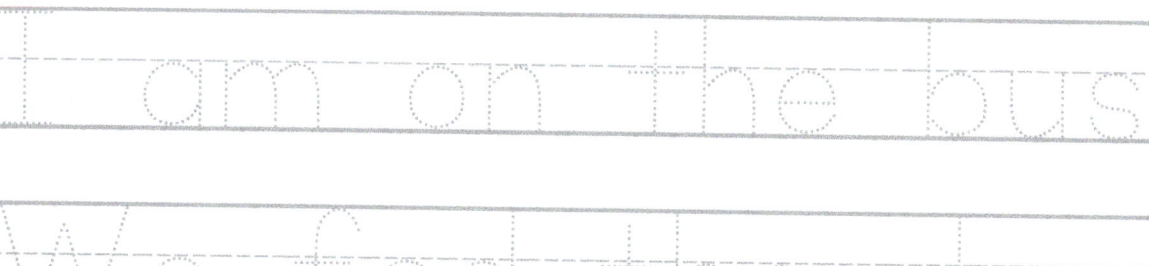

We fed the dog.

Read the sentences you have written.

CHEETAH® reward stickers

MARVELOUS!

SPECTACULAR!

YOU
NAILED
IT!

SHINE ON!

YOU
NAILED
IT!

BRILLIANT
EFFORT!

1
YOU DID IT!

GREAT!

GREAT
TRY!

KEEP
TRYING!

Did you have fun? I did!

This page is left blank
so you can cut out the reward
stickers.

Set 5

/j/, long ī, or, long ō and /z/

Here are some C-DER books to read:

Sound	C-DER reference	Book title
long i	Set 4, Book 33	*Riding My Bike*
long o	Set 6, Book 47	*Sam's Boat*
z	Set 3, Book 22	*Party Time!*

Let's read together: Visiting Aunt Jen and Uncle Joe

Before you begin ask, "*Who do you like to visit in your family? Why do you like to visit them?*"

During the story, stop before reading page 12. Ask, "*Who do you think this man is? Why do you think that?*"

After the story ask, "*What happened in the story? How is it the same when you visit your family? How is it different?*"

CHEETAH® train loves a song, zooming as it hums along.
Uncle John loves a joke, laughing with the jolly folk.
Can you guess which sound is next?

Find an instrument, then play and sing along using the lyrics above!
Watch in a mirror as you make my sound!

J is on the way to town.
CHEETAH® train is slowing down.

Jj

Listen as an adult says the words. Colour the objects with a /j/ sound.

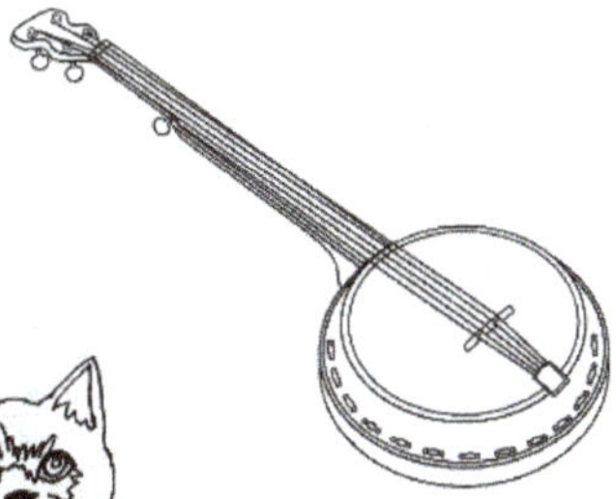

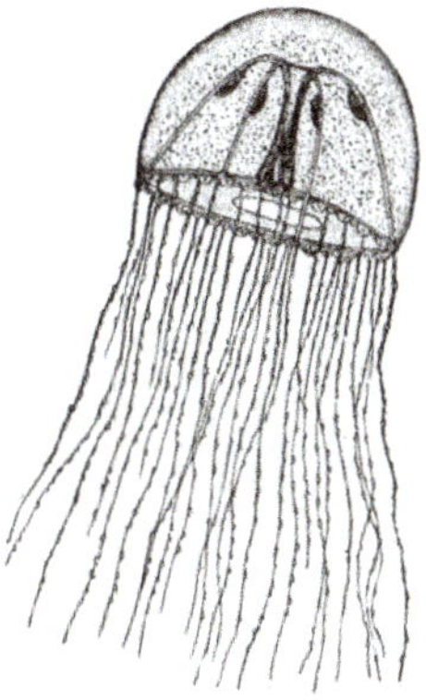

Practise writing the letter *j*.

Listen then <u>underline</u> all the words in the passage with the /j/ sound.

Jen's family is big and jolly.

"I have three jolly brothers," she says.

We play and enjoy a joke together.

"With my family, every day is joyful," Jen says.

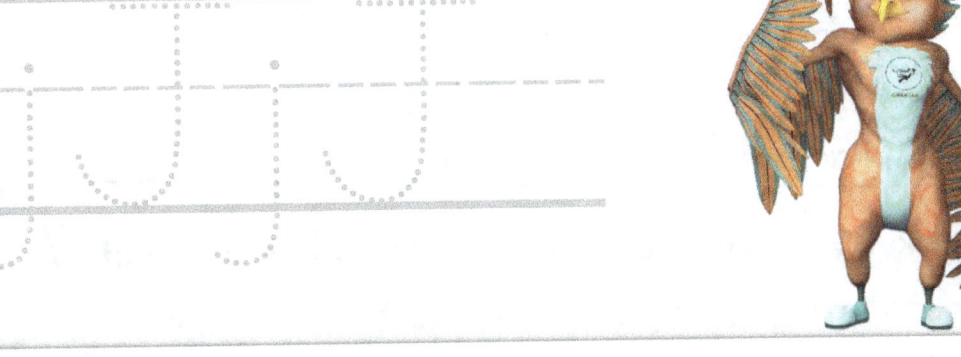

Colour the face that shows how you feel about the /j/ sound.

Got it! | Almost got it | No, didn't get it

You are growing all the time. Keep spreading your wings!

Dear Parent: Date: ________________

_______________ does/does not fully understand the phonic sound /j/. Please continue to review at home.

Signed: ______________________

Dear Teacher: Date:______________

Thank you. We have reviewed the phonic sound /j/ together. My child had a chance to teach me.

Signed: _____________________

Reward sticker for parent or guardian goes here.

Great job!

____

(write name)

understands the phonic sound /j/.

Sticker for pupil goes here!

Let's read together: Riding My Bike

Before you begin ask, "*Can you ride a bike? What is fun about riding a bike? What might be dangerous about riding a bike?*"

During the story, stop after the first page. Ask, "*Who are the characters in this story? What do you think they might be like?*"

After the story ask, "*What did we find out about the characters in this story?*" Reread together to look for answers.

CHEETAH® train loves a song, zooming as it hums along.
Mike is on his bike. He wants to fly his kite tonight.
Can you guess which sound is next?

Find an instrument, then play and sing along using the lyrics above!
Can you make my sound 3 times?

I is on the way to town.
CHEETAH® train is slowing down.

Ii ie ig
i_e y

Read the words. Colour the pies with a long ī sound.

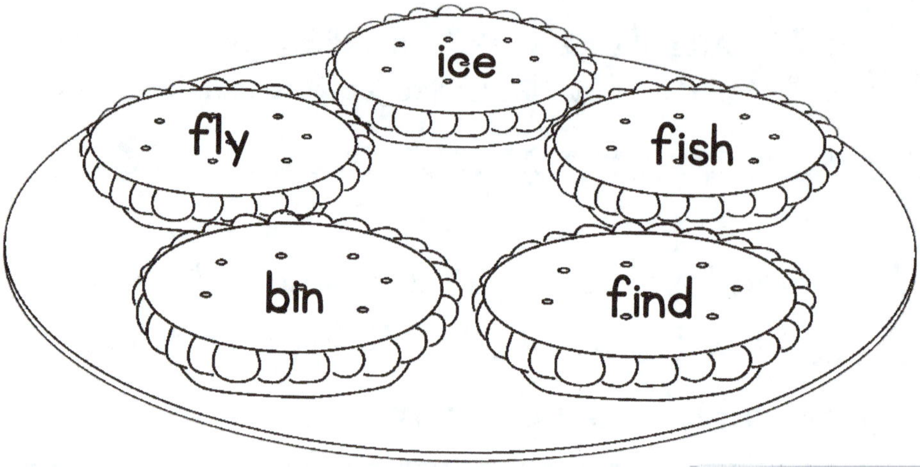

Practise writing the letter *i* and *e*.

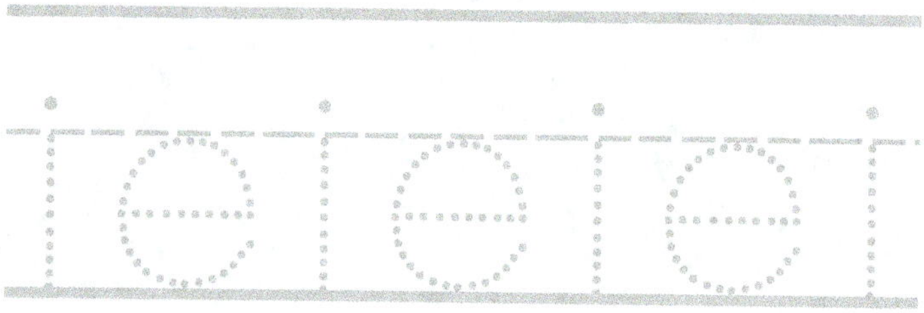

When I see 2 vowel friends,
the first one is rude and
always talks first!!

Listen then underline all the words in the passage with the long ī sound.

Iris saw a spider under a pile of paper.

She cried, "Quick! Hide!"

"The spider is tiny!" Mike said. "I have an idea."

"I will hide him in my hands and take him outside."

Colour the face that shows how you feel about the long ī sound.

Got it! | Almost got it | No, didn't get it

If you are not sure, ask for help.

Dear Parent: Date: _______________

_____________ does/does not fully understand the phonic sound long ī. Please continue to review at home.

Signed: ____________________

Dear Teacher: Date:____________

Thank you. We have reviewed the phonic sound long ī together. My child had a chance to teach me.

Signed: ___________________

Reward sticker for parent or guardian goes here.

Nice work!

____

(write name)

understands the phonic sound /f/.

Sticker for pupil goes here!

Let's read together: It's Wet Outside

Before you begin ask, "*What do you do when it is wet outside?*"

During the story, stop after reading page 5. *Ask, "Do you know what the word 'seek' means?"* Reread and read on, modelling how to look for clues together.

After the story, write a sentence to answer the final question of the story: "*What do you do when outside is wet?*"

CHEETAH® train loves a song, zooming as it hums along.
The farm is near the port. Sam can hear the horses snort.
Can you guess which sound is next?

Find an instrument, then play and sing along using the lyrics above!
What shape is your mouth as you make our sound?

Or is on the way to town.
CHEETAH® train is slowing down.

or

Read the words and draw lines to match them to the pictures.

horse fork corn port

Practise writing the letter *o* and *r*

Good for you!

or or

or or

Listen then <u>underline</u> all the words in the passage with the /or/ sound.

Every morning, I help more and more.

I take a mop and clean the floor.

I set the table with forks for dinner.

Let's eat some corn! It's a winner!

Colour the face that shows how you feel about the or sound.

Got it! | Almost got it | No, didn't get it

The more you learn, the more you soar!

Dear Parent: Date: _______________

_______________ does/does not fully understand the phonic sound /or/. Please continue to review at home.

Signed: ______________________

Dear Teacher: Date: _____________

Thank you. We have reviewed the phonic sound /or/ together. My child had a chance to teach me.

Signed: ____________________

Reward sticker for parent or guardian goes here.

Good for you!

____

(write name

understands the phonic sound /or/.

Sticker for pupil goes here!

CHEETAH® Purrrrrrr Publishing
presents
Sam's Boat
Level 2
Set 5,
Book 41
Bernadette Vidal
Paulette Trowers, JD
C-DER™
CHEETAH Decodable
& Early Readers

Let's read together: Sam's Boat

Before you begin ask, "*Do you have a toy boat? Have you ever made a toy boat yourself? How might you make one?*"

During the story, stop after reading the first page. Ask, "*What is the problem in this story? Why might Sam's boat not float?*"

After the story ask, "*What was wrong with Sam's boat? Who helped him to fix it? How was the problem solved?*"

CHEETAH® train loves a song, zooming as it hums along.
Jojo wants to go, go go, over bridges high and low.
Can you guess which sound is next?

Find an instrument, then play and sing along using the lyrics above!
Round your lips into an 'o' shape.

O is on the way to town.
CHEETAH® train is slowing down.

Listen as an adult says the word. Write the missing letters to complete each word.

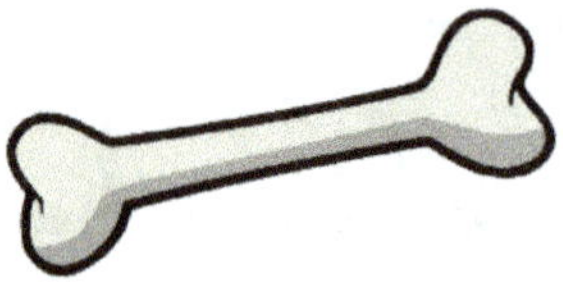

b _ n _

b _ _

s _ _

Practise writing the letters *o* and *a*.

o a o a

o a o a

Listen then <u>underline</u> all the words in the passage with the long ō sound.

At school, Flo held a show with her toy robot.

"It can dance and sing. Watch it go!"

The children clapped and cheered, "Go, Flo! Go!"

She smiled. "I play with it over and over, you know!

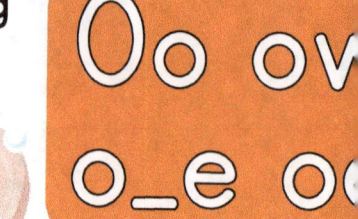

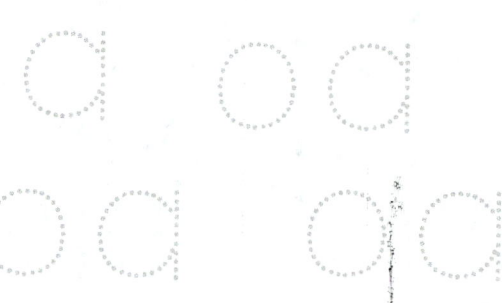

Colour the face that shows how you feel about the long ō sound.

Got it!
Almost got it
No, didn't get it

You can do it! Keep flying and trying!

Dear Parent: Date: ________________

_______________ does/does not fully understand the long / sound. Please continue to review at home.

Signed: ______________________

Dear Teacher: Date:______________

Thank you. We have reviewed the long phonic sound ō together. My child had a chance to teach me.

Signed: ______________________

Reward sticker for parent or guardian goes here.

Go for it!

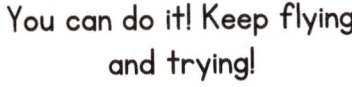

____

(write name

understands the phonic sound long ō.

Sticker for pupil goes here!

Let's read together: Party Time!

Before you begin ask, "*What can you do if you do not know what a word means?*" Discuss context cues and the use of a dictionary.

During the story, stop after reading each page to ask, "*Were there any words you did not understand?*" Model how to find out the meaning.

After the story, read again without pausing. Ask, "*Can you retell the story?*"

CHEETAH® train loves a song, zooming as it hums along.
Baz the bee is flying free, buzzing over land and sea.
Can you guess which sound is next?

Find an instrument, then play and sing along using the lyrics above!
Can you feel the vibration as you make my sound?

Z is on the way to town.
CHEETAH® train is slowing down.

Zz Ss

Write the correct word from the box under the picture.

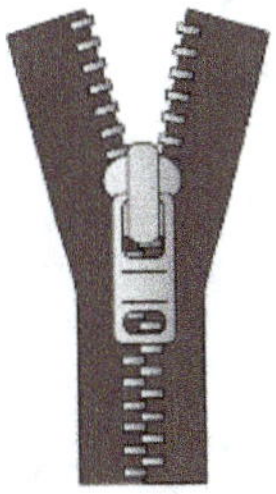

rose	maze	zip

Practise writing the letter *z*.

Amazing!!

Listen then underline all the words in the passage with the /z/ sound.

My jacket's zipper is so noisy.

Every time I zip it up, it sounds like music.

"Please can you fix it?" I asked my mother.

My mother is always there to help me.

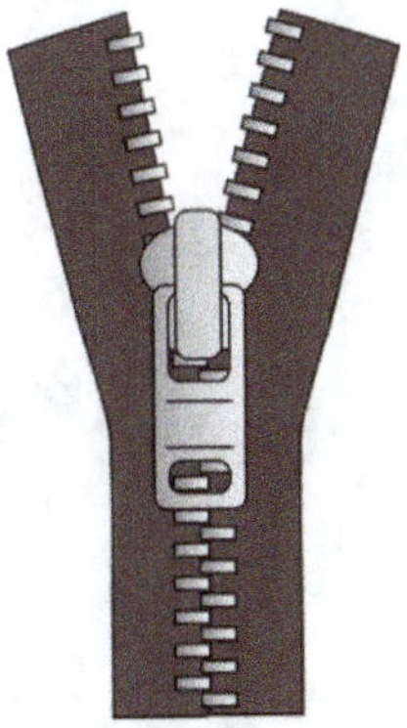

Colour the face that shows how you feel about the /z/ sound.

Got it!
Almost got it
No, didn't get it

What new things will you learn today? There is so much to find out!

Dear Parent: Date: _______________

_______________ does/does not fully understand the phonic sound /z/. Please continue to review at home.

Signed: ______________________

Dear Teacher: Date:______________

Thank you. We have reviewed the phonic sound /z/ together. My child had a chance to teach me.

Signed: ____________________

Reward sticker for parent or guardian goes here.

Amazing!

____

(write name

understands the phonic sound /z/.

Sticker for pupil goes here!

CHEETAH®'s review

Choose the word from the box to complete each sentence.

or	jump	go	rose	white

I can ____ very high.

The moon is _____.

Would you like this __ that?

It is time to __ to sleep.

Look at the red ____ grow.

Use the letters to make as many long i and long o words as you can. Letters can be used more than once, and nonsense words are welcome. Be creative and have fun!

e k c i o l b t

Nonsense words are made up and have no real meaning e.g. lib

CHEETAH's review

Find the high frequency words in the wordsearch.

o	r	g	o	m
j	u	m	p	u
u	a	c	e	o
s	f	i	n	d
t	b	s	p	s

find   jump   go   open   just   is   or

Use the picture clues to complete the crossword.

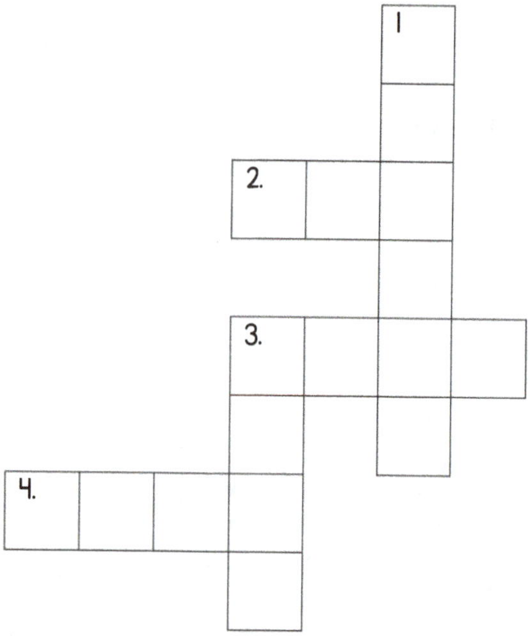

Down:

1. 

3. 

Across:

2. 

3. 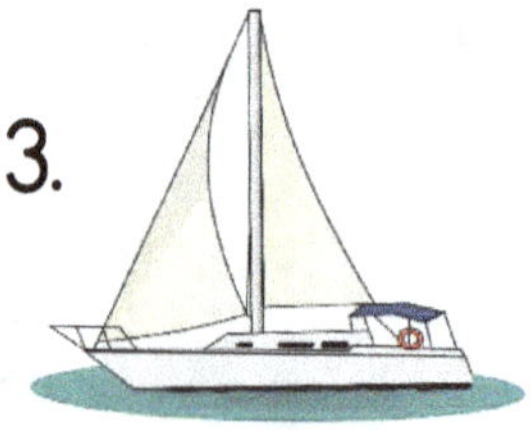

4. 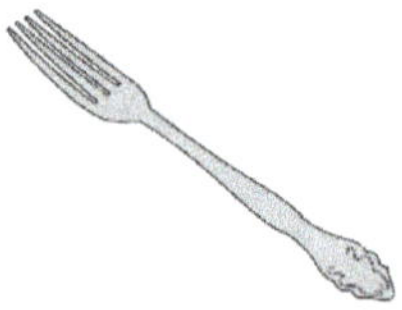

CHEETAH® Purrrrrr Publishing

Presents

Set 5

A Fun Day

j, l, or, long o, z

A CHEETAH® Poster Story

Jack woke up Jen.

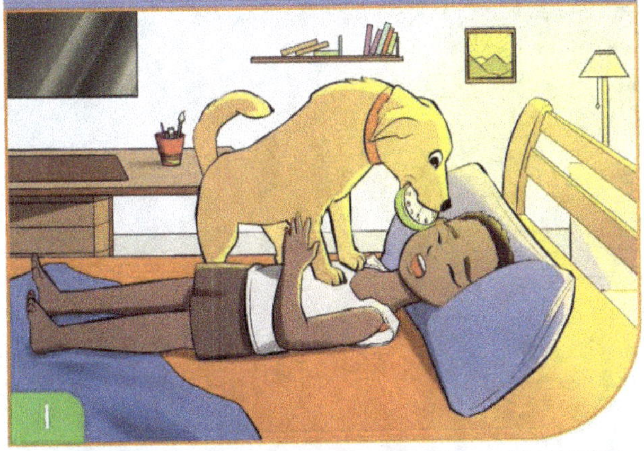

Jen and Jack hope to have a fun day! "Zip up the sack, Jack," said Jen.

Time to go for a hike.

Jen and Jack fly kites!

"Is there more time to play?" said Jen.

Jack can ride a bike with Jen.

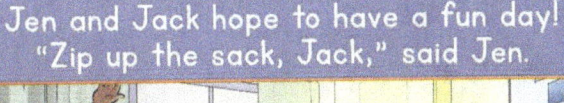

Set 5

A Fun Day

A CHEETAH® Poster Story

j, l, or, long o, z

Time to dine on corn with lime.

Have a bite of jam with the corn.

Look at the bugs buzz by the jam!

Jen will tell a joke to Jack.

It is late. Time to go home!

Jack and Jen zig zag back home.

Let's create

Complete the table. Put the letters together to make words.

beginning sound	middle sound	end sound	words created
		t	
j	i	g	
z	o	p	
		r	

List the words that you do not know the meaning of.

____

____

Ask an adult what they mean.

Sound out the words you have made.

Let's put together

Connect the boxes to make words from the -ug word family. Write them in the given space.

j
b
h
d
_ug

____

____

____

____

What other words belong to this word family?

Let's take apart

Break each word into sounds. Write the sounds in the boxes.

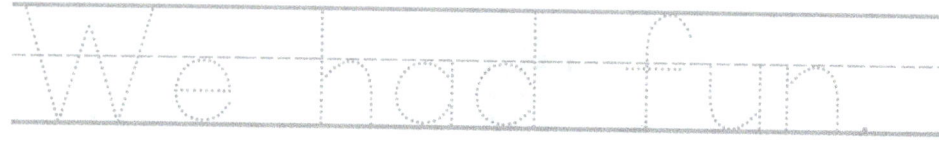

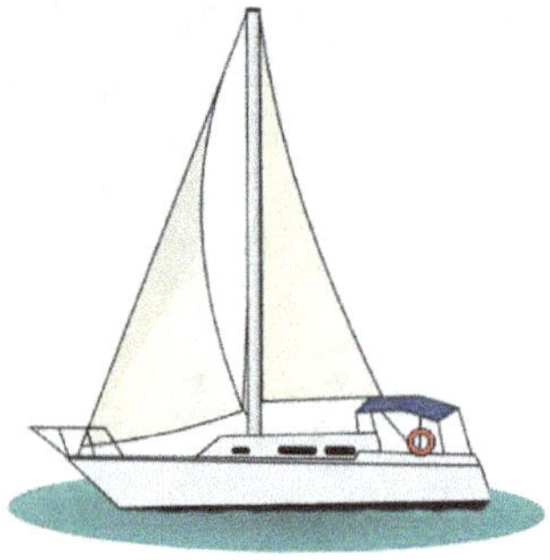

Two letters sometimes make a single sound.

Let's trace

Trace the letters to write sentences.

I like the ball.

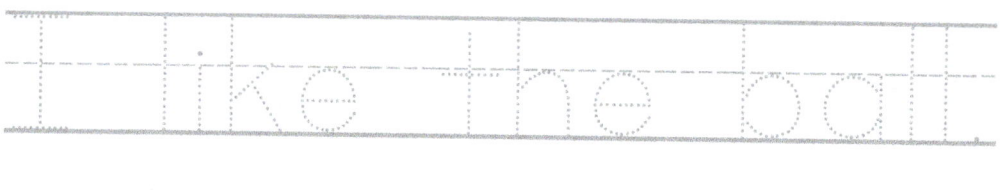

We had fun.

Read the sentences you have written.

CHEETAH® reward stickers

MARVELOUS!
SPECTACULAR!
YOU NAILED IT!
SHINE ON!
YOU NAILED IT!
BRILLIANT EFFORT!
YOU DID IT!
1
GREAT!
GREAT TRY!
KEEP TRYING!

Did you have fun? I did!

This page is left blank
so you can cut out the reward
stickers.

www.ingramcontent.com/pod-product-compliance
Lightning Source LLC
Chambersburg PA
CBHW081336120626
46546CB00011B/3369
* 9 7 8 1 9 6 4 2 4 3 6 4 1 *